THE IMAGE OF LEADERSHIP
IN REAL ESTATE

Special Edition, 10th Anniversary

THE IMAGE OF LEADERSHIP IN REAL ESTATE

How Leaders in Real Estate Package Themselves
to Stand Out for All the Right Reasons

by
Sylvie di Giusto

Copyright © 2024 Sylvie di Giusto LLC
All rights reserved

No part of this book may be reproduced in any form or by any electronic or mechanical means, including information storage and retrieval systems, without permission in writing from the author. The only exception is by a reviewer, who may quote short excerpts in a published review.

The information presented herein represents the views of the author as of the date of publication. This book is presented for informational purposes only. Because of the rate at which conditions change, the author reserves the right to alter and update her opinions at any time. Although every attempt has been made to verify the information in this book, the author does not assume any responsibility for errors, inaccuracies, or omissions.

ISBN: 979-8-9901927-2-0

To the place-makers and dream-weavers,
whose dedication to finding homes and spaces
creates lasting legacies and thriving environments.

Contents

About This Special Edition 9

Foreword by Caroline K. Huo 13

Introduction 17

Chapter 1: Seven Seconds 22
The Cost of a Poor Professional Identity 32
Shaping Your Narrative with Intention 39
The Science of First Impressions 42
The Sustained Imprint 45
The Invisible Filters of Perception 49
Standing Out for the Right Reasons 58
When Details Speak Loudest 61

Chapter 2: Your Professional Identity 68
The ABCDEs of Your Professional Identity 75
Internal and External Consistency 81
From Shadows to the Spotlight 85

Chapter 3: Leaders Look Confident 92
Leaders Are Confident about Their Body 99
Leaders Are Confident about Their Age 105
Leaders Are Confident about Their Gender Identity 107
Leaders Are Confident about Their Style 111

Chapter 4: Leaders Look Authentic 116
Keywords Are the Keys to Authenticity 121
The Explorer: Approachable and Relaxed 125
The Traditionalist: Trustworthy and Reliable 127
The Cosmopolitan: Sophisticated and Eloquent 129
The Caregiver: Supportive and Nurturing 132
The Avant-Garde: Individualistic and Creative 134
The Glamorous: Magnetic and Extravagant 137
The Dramatic: Strong and Fearless 139

Chapter 5: Leaders Look Professional 144
Prescribed Uniformity in Action 151
Silent Standards and Unwritten Uniforms 153
Internal Mandates We Self-Enforce 157
Dressing Beyond the Code: Situational Awareness 163

Chapter 6: Leaders Look Respectful 168
It's a Sign of Self-Respect 170
It Shows You Respect Others 173
It's Not Always Reciprocated 177
Damage Control: When Things Go Wrong 180

Chapter 7: Leaders Look Controlled 186
Self-Awareness and Self-Reflection: Controlling Your Inner Compass 187
Self-Care and Self-Discipline: Controlling Your Well-Being 189
Self-Improvement and Self-Promotion: Controlling Your Narrative 190
Be Prepared for the Predictable and the Unpredictable 192
It's Not Only about Clothes 193

Chapter 8: Leadership in a Digital Landscape 200
KNOW: Assessing the Scope of Your e-Shadow 203
REPAIR: Correcting Your Cyber Image 206
OWN: Claiming Your Virtual Real Estate 207
CONTROL: Commanding Your Digital Boundaries 209
MONITOR: Persistent Surveillance of Your Online Self 210

Chapter 9: Leaders Lead by Example 214
The Leader's Challenge: It's Not You, It's Someone Else 217

Chapter 10: Moving Forward 228

Acknowledgments 233

About the Author 235

Perception Audit 236

Your Voice and Our Collective Reach 237

About This Special Edition

Ten years ago, I released my first-ever book, *The Image of Leadership*, not fully grasping the impact it would have on my own career trajectory. At that time, I remember feeling a mix of excitement and nervousness. After all, releasing a book into the world is no small feat. Just a few weeks before I hit that "Publish" button, and while I was still overthinking every single word, Mark Sanborn, a titan of leadership thought, bestselling author, and Hall of Fame speaker himself, gave me a piece of advice that has stayed with me: "Nobody cares about your first book, Sylvie, but everybody cares that you have a first book." You know, in the speaking world, a book is an entry point, a business card, a conversation starter—a testament to your thoughts and expertise. So off I went and finally published it.

That first book did indeed open doors, sparked conversations, and led to speaking engagements, fulfilling its role perfectly—and much more. But Mark wasn't finished after his original words. He turned around and, while walking off, threw a greater challenge my way: "But you really must write a good second book, Sylvie." So consider this updated and expanded edition of *The Image of Leadership for Real Estate Leaders* my "second good book," the refined version of my initial offering, now tailored to the unique challenges and opportunities of the real estate industry.

You see, a lot has changed in ten years, and the real estate world is no exception. The digital landscape has evolved rapidly, transforming the way real estate leaders work and connect with clients. The global marketplace has become increasingly interconnected, requiring real estate leaders to navigate cultural differences and build international relationships daily. And we can't forget the profound impact of the pandemic, shifting market trends, changing consumer preferences, and new regulations, which have reshaped the real estate landscape. For a while, it was clear that *The Image of Leadership* needed more than just a touch-up—it needed a full makeover to reflect these seismic shifts and provide guidance for real estate leaders navigating this new landscape. It needed a comprehensive renewal to stay relevant in a world that has fundamentally shifted.

And so I embarked on a journey of complete revision rather than mere superficial changes. This wasn't just about updating; it was about reimagining and realigning the book with the times we live in, all through the lens of leadership.

While the original structure and focus of the book remained, over the past ten years I also had the privilege of speaking to a variety of real estate leaders. And you know, as a keynote speaker, the exchange is a two-way street. For every insight I've offered from the stage, I've received an equal measure of wisdom from my audiences. The specific challenges they've shared, the questions they've asked, and the stories they've told have deepened my understanding of the unique demands of leadership in the real estate industry. I'm immensely thankful for this reciprocal learning. It's this exchange that has breathed new life into *The Image of Leadership*, transforming it into an edition that reflects not just my voice but also the collective wisdom of the many dedicated real estate professionals I've engaged with.

So, here's to you, the real estate leaders, who embody resilience and dedication every day. This book is for you—the ethical, the passionate, the determined—no matter if you are a tenacious real estate agent making your first deal or a visionary brokerage executive steering your firm to new heights. Whether you are a leader in residential real estate, commercial property management, industrial real estate, or land development, this is your guide for navigating the high stakes and unique challenges of your professional journey, no matter your specific role.

It's a thank-you for your service across the real estate industry and a tool to aid your journey forward, whether you're engaging with clients face-to-face, over the phone, or online. It's a recognition of the real estate leaders who are shaping the future of the industry, one transaction at a time.

Consider this book the "second" that Mark Sanborn urged me to perfect—a version refined by experience and honed by the passage of time—a handbook for the present, a road map for the future, and a testament to the enduring power of a real estate leader's professional identity.

May this updated and extended edition serve you as a compass through the ever-changing landscape of leadership, inspiring you to continue making impactful decisions with confidence, purpose, and authority as you navigate the unique challenges of interacting with clients and driving success in your role as a leader for your team.

Foreword
by Caroline K. Huo

Early in my career, I recall a pivotal moment when I realized the profound impact of first impressions and the importance of leading oneself. I was meeting a high-profile client for the first time, the head of a major department at Stanford University Hospital. He was a BIG deal, like... huge. Being newer to the industry, I worked myself up into a frenzy. My grandmother had taught me from a young age, "Dress appropriately so you are not embarrassed if you bump into the President in the elevator. Carry yourself with confidence even when you are not. When pushed, do not back down from what you believe." I had heeded her advice for many years, until that evening.

I was not confident, I was uncomfortable, I agreed when I should not have, I did not show my expertise, and to top it off, my jacket, which I had purchased for this special meeting on sale from Nordstrom Rack, was too big and made me look like I was twelve.

I wasn't me, and I certainly wasn't the confident professional the referrer told him about. I let my fear derail me from presenting myself effectively and authentically. Looking back, I lost the listing even before I stepped through the front door, and I did not have the understanding of how I could have prevented it.

Through my over twenty years of personal experience in residential real estate, leading The Caroline K. Huo Group and various offices, teaching around the world, observing, and interviewing other leaders (in and out of the world of real estate) in my role as Keller Williams Luxury's Director of Professional Development for Keller Williams Realty International, co-leading KW's Luxury Division with Brady Sandahl, the Director of Growth, I have learned many things. I was overwhelmed with gratitude when I realized that what I had wished I had known twenty years ago is now in the pages of this one magical book. It is not just about how we dress or present ourselves; it is about the consistency, integrity, and authenticity that we bring to every single interaction, whether in person or online. Our image is a silent ambassador, speaking volumes before we utter a single word. Sylvie encapsulates concepts and practices that are crucial for any real estate professional aiming not just to excel but to thrive, to be different, to stand out, and to elevate our industry in the eyes of the public.

Being invited to write this foreword for Sylvie di Giusto, the dynamic thought leader and international speaker on leadership whom I admire greatly, is an opportunity to shout from the rooftops why this book, "The Image of Leadership in Real Estate," is needed and appropriate now, at this moment when the relevance of the professional agent is being questioned.

Over the past few years, the real estate industry has seen significant changes in the concept of real estate agents and real estate leaders. In an era where influencers are often seen as "real estate leaders" based on clicks and likes rather than credibility, this book emphasizes the importance of authentic leadership and professional integrity, helping real estate professionals stand out to confirm, and own, our relevance.

In the pages that follow, Sylvie demonstrates how making intentional decisions can shape perceptions, behaviors, and outcomes. Yes, you can affect outcomes! She offers insights into the context and content of how to embrace and relay what makes you uniquely you, in all that is seen and all that is unseen. She emphasizes the ABCDEs of your professional identity, and how looking confident, looking authentic, looking professional, looking respectful, and looking controlled is enveloped in that identity.

She addresses how to lead effectively in the digital landscape and, when leading others, the necessity and significance of leading by example. Sylvie's perspective, combined with tactical advice such as how to talk with your team if they are not aligned with this vision, provide valuable guidance for both seasoned leaders and those aspiring to make their mark in real estate. As they say, "To lead others, you must first lead yourself," and this book is the guide.

Written for all, I was particularly impressed that Sylvie took the time to address gender and the role of women in real estate. According to Realtor.com and NAR, women constitute the majority of the real estate workforce, particularly in residential real estate, but they are underrepresented in leadership positions. The majority of residential real estate agents are women. However, when it comes to leadership roles, the numbers are less balanced, even less so in commercial real estate.

Despite this, the presence of influential female leaders in real estate is growing, as seen in the increasing number of women featured in power rankings and leadership lists. To ensure the continued growth and success of our industry, I encourage everyone to support and mentor emerging leaders, regardless of gender or gender identity, and to advocate for equitable opportunities in all areas of real estate. By fostering an inclusive and diverse leadership environment, we can collectively raise the standards of our profession and inspire future generations.

Whether you are an individual agent or someone who leads a team, brokerage, or corporation, whether you are in residential real estate or sell skyscrapers, this book opens your eyes to how you can make conscious choices that impact how others perceive you before meeting you, how to show up in a way that is aligned with your digital presence and reputation, and how they, and those you lead, experience you.

"The Image of Leadership in Real Estate" is not just a book; it is a call to action for all of us to elevate our standards, refine our image, and inspire trust and confidence in those we serve.

By doing so, you will not only elevate your own leadership but also contribute to the advancement of the real estate industry as a whole. You have the power of choice to affect your outcome, and once you make that choice, Sylvie will show you how.

Here's to your journey of becoming an exemplary real estate leader. Here's to Your Excellence!

Caroline K. Huo
Director of Professional Development, Keller Williams Luxury

Introduction

Welcome to this special edition of *The Image of Leadership for Real Estate Leaders*. The title reflects the reality that every leader must acknowledge, which is that true leadership manifests itself in ways that are both seen and unseen. They're equally important. Even though all leaders have their own individual styles and personalities, it cannot be doubted that the most effective leaders who succeed over a long period of time are seen and accepted because their interior skills and exterior images are in perfect alignment. In other words, what you see is what you get. As leaders, they're consistent and dependable, and their professional identity—which I'll introduce to you later in the book—is intentional, strong, and durable.

You may possibly wonder, is this book really for me? My answer is a resounding yes. Be it navigating the fast-paced world of residential real estate, managing complex commercial properties, overseeing industrial spaces, or specializing in land development, this book is crafted for real estate leaders across all sectors, regardless of their specific niche or role.

Whether you're part of a large brokerage, an independent agent, or the founder of your own real estate venture, the insights and strategies shared here will illuminate your path to success. It doesn't matter if you're just starting out in your real estate journey, already leading a team of agents, or steering your brokerage to new heights as a top executive—this book is designed to instill a culture of excellence at every stage of your career.

The core principle remains the same: no matter where you are in your real estate journey or what segment of the industry you serve, the way you present yourself should consistently reflect the leader you aspire to be. The challenges you face may differ—from mastering the art of client relationships to navigating complex market dynamics—but the importance of a strong professional identity remains constant.

This book is your compass, guiding you toward solidifying your professional identity and shaping a compelling leadership narrative that will serve you throughout your real estate career. It will take you step by step through the development of this professional identity. The focus will be on all those things people perceive about you, with an emphasis on your "look of leadership."

I mean your image, what others see and experience, as you lead a client meeting, speak at an industry conference, or articulate your market insights in an interview. It's based on the proven concept that you cannot simply tell others you're a leader and expect them to treat you as one. You have to show others your leadership, every day, consistently, and in a way that encourages them to instantly accept you as someone in whom they will place their trust.

While this book focuses in parts on the way you represent yourself internally to your team, I want to remind you that all those principles, of course, also hold true when interacting with external stakeholders. As a real estate leader, you are always "on stage," not just in team meetings or when facing your own upper management. Every interaction matters; whether it's with a client on a property tour, a potential referral partner at an industry event, or when collaborating with investors, lenders, and financial institutions to secure the best deals for your clients. Your professional identity also comes into play when working with contractors and vendors to ensure the smooth execution of real estate transactions and property management. And even when you are "off" work, interacting with your community, your professional identity continues to shape perceptions.

Remember, everyone is watching you, all the time, and your interactions in every situation contribute to the overall perception of your leadership. Only by being mindful of this can you ensure that your professional identity is cohesive, consistent, and impactful, no matter the context or setting.

We'll begin with the seven-second rule. This is that critical moment when others first encounter you. They may have some prior knowledge of you, but this is the first time they actually lay eyes on you. I'll show you how others make up their minds very quickly about your leadership potential and either open the door for you or slam it shut. The good thing is that this process is entirely under your control. Already within these first micro-moments, you can choose to present yourself as a real estate leader or not.

We'll then dive into the powerful undercurrents of the human mind and explore how others are already heavily influenced after those initial micro-moments, shaping their perceptions and decisions in profound ways. However, these dynamics can be influenced by you using tools that you already have. Hence, I'll reveal the components of your professional presence—the ABCDEs of your professional identity: appearance, behavior, communication, digital footprint, and environment.

While all components of the ABCDEs are crucial and only work effectively when they intersect and interplay, we'll focus on how you are perceived visually. However, this is not a fashion guide. I'm not going to detail specific items of clothing or accessories you need to buy or wear. What I want to provide for you is a deep understanding of the concepts you need to put into practice in your own way. I want to give you the power to create your own professional identity that is true to your personality, that works for you for the duration of your real estate career, and that also stands as a testament to the brokerage or agency you're a part of and, by extension, the real estate industry you work in as a whole.

We'll also delve deeper into the area of your digital leadership. In an age where your digital presence is as crucial as your in-person interactions, we'll explore how to cultivate a compelling digital footprint that reinforces your leadership identity. From leveraging social media platforms to crafting a powerful online narrative, you'll learn strategies to control and extend your influence and establish yourself as a thought leader in the digital sphere.

While this book is focused on helping you refine your professional identity, you'll also become aware that some of your team members may struggle to apply the elements of their ABCDEs effectively. As you read through the pages, you'll find yourself identifying areas where you and your team can grow together. For addressing these sensitive issues with team members, I'll equip you with techniques to approach these difficult conversations with confidence and grace. You'll learn how to communicate with empathy, assert your authority when necessary, and foster a culture of open and constructive dialogue within your team because, as a leader, your success is intrinsically tied to your ability to inspire and guide others. Hence, we'll explore the art of leading by example, showcasing how your decisions set the tone for your entire team and your brokerage. Only by embodying the qualities you seek to instill in others will you create a ripple effect of positive change.

In crafting this book, it was important to me to recognize that real estate leaders' experiences and identities are vast and diverse. This book is committed to embracing every real estate leader, regardless of their background or the unique challenges they face in their specific role or niche. Here, every real estate leader is welcome and valued because leaders come in all genders, shapes, sizes, ages, styles, and levels—including yours.

I hope this book will help you develop your professional identity on your journey of becoming the real estate leader you deserve to be. It's all a matter of letting others see your inner star that is ready to shine.

So let's get started on this exciting journey toward achieving your full leadership potential.

Love,

Sylvie

Chapter 1
Seven Seconds

Seven Seconds:
Just a Glimpse, but the Vision Lasts.
1 2 3 4 5 6 7

Chapter 1:
Seven Seconds

Appearance matters. Every hour of every day, we humans evaluate our environment based on what we see and hear. We avoid situations and individuals that seem threatening. We gravitate toward situations and individuals that appear welcoming. When we meet someone, we use sensory information to quickly determine if we're going to get along with them or if we need to keep our distance. We turn on the television and say, "This show looks good. I think I'll watch it." At the store, we inspect the food we want to buy. When a dog approaches us on the street, before we extend our hand we examine its body language. Is the tail wagging or is the dog tense?

Similarly, we walk into team meetings and instantly assess the room, evaluating the body language and expressions of all participants. We open the door for a home tour and instantly assume we know we've got a deal, or not, with a potential buyer based on their initial reactions. We visit a vacant lot with a developer and judge their initial enthusiasm based on their vision and excitement for the project. We step onto a stage to give a real estate market presentation and scan the audience to read their reactions. We enter a networking event and quickly decide who seems approachable and who might be more challenging to engage.

We all do it—me and you—whether we want to, whether we are aware of it, or even if we think we are above it.

Just as we judge others, we're judged by the people who meet us or see us. Do we appear trustworthy? Confident? Or do we appear uncertain or detached? Are we seen as decisive and capable of guiding a client through a complex real estate transaction? Do we project an image of approachability that encourages open communication and collaboration?

These initial perceptions will then further influence the decisions people make about us. Should they hire us as their real estate agent? Refer us to their friends and family? Trust us with their most significant financial investment?

Research supports this idea. Some studies suggest it takes as little as milliseconds or three, seven, or eleven seconds to delineate different characteristics you're judged on. In my professional work, I've focused on the study that implies it takes place within seven seconds. These seven seconds and the research I rely on in my work is based on a study conducted by psychologist Dr. Michael Solomon at NYU. It suggests our initial imprint is not based on a single element; instead, it is a composite of at least eleven different elements that others subconsciously judge within those first moments of meeting us. These elements are as follows:

1. Socioeconomic level
2. Education level
3. Competence and honesty, believability, and perceived credibility
4. Sex role identification
5. Level of sophistication
6. Trustworthiness
7. Level of success
8. Ethnicity
9. Religious background
10. Political background
11. Social/sexual/professional desirability

Yet it's imperative to approach this list with a discerning mind.

On one enlightening occasion, I had the honor of engaging with Dr. Solomon in a conversation, and he shared a significant point with me: like many scientific findings, the interpretations of his study have been bent to fit various narratives across the internet and by self-proclaimed experts. It's one of those pervasive myths that human judgment rigidly conforms to this eleven-elements-and-seven-seconds rule. Yet the study never confirmed this assumption and has consistently been taken out of context. He went so far as to share that the study, as it is nowadays described on the internet, never took place in the way it is portrayed. A powerful reminder for all of us to not take information from the internet at face value and to always verify the original sources.

So, while I won't delve into the specifics of the study or its misrepresentations found online, it's important to understand the broader implication; regardless of which research you look at, they all have one thing in common: this process occurs automatically in our brains—whether we're aware of it, whether we find it fair, or whether, under our shabby clothes, we have the soul of Mother Theresa.

Think about it this way: when a client meets you for the first time, they're not instantly evaluating your real estate skills or your market insights. They're evaluating you as a person. They're asking themselves, "Is this someone I can trust? Is this someone who understands my needs? Is this someone who is professional, knowledgeable, and reliable?" Before a client makes the decision to work with you as their real estate agent, they first need to "buy into you."

Your look of leadership provides the first clues to answering those questions. Of course, appearance alone isn't enough. You also need to have the substance to back it up. This means demonstrating your expertise, reliability, and value through various actions over time, shown by your deep understanding of the real estate market, your ability to ask insightful questions and provide tailored solutions, your prompt and effective follow-up, and your commitment to exceeding client expectations.

But in those crucial first moments, your appearance sets the stage for the relationship. It's the foundation upon which trust is built.

Anyone who aspires to a position of leadership in any capacity needs to understand the power of their visual presence. The good news is that this is something you can control. You can make it what you want.

Let's start with a story. It's about two real estate professionals, Sarah and Emily, who are aiming for a key client contract. They're competing to be the listing agent for a high-end property owned by a couple, Mark and Lisa—a deal that represents a major opportunity in their respective careers.

First, let's meet Sarah. Brimming with the anticipation of securing the listing, she waits in the sleek lobby of the couple's upscale condo building. Lisa arrives to greet her. With a confident smile that's both friendly and businesslike, she shakes Sarah's hand with a firm grip before leading her toward the condo.

As they walk through the building's luxurious common areas, past the concierge desk and the residents' lounge, there's a thoughtful, yet uncomfortable, silence between Sarah and Lisa. Upon arriving at the condo, Lisa gestures for Sarah to take a seat. She then moves to the other side of the living room, and with a brief smile, she begins discussing the property with her husband Mark, who has been waiting for them. Their questions are straightforward. Their inquiries are pointed, delving into Sarah's past successes and exploring the distinctive skills she would bring to marketing their property.

During the meeting, Sarah has an uneasy feeling. She doesn't think she's connecting with Mark and Lisa. Her credentials are solid—her track record is what secured her this invitation—but she senses the couple is seeking something more—or something else. She feels the opportunity slipping away, like water through her fingers. She can't quite pinpoint the issue. Maybe, she speculates, Mark and Lisa are simply methodical and reserved by nature.

After twenty minutes, Lisa closes her notebook and looks up. "Well then, do you have any questions for us?" Sarah has a multitude of questions, but Lisa's composed conduct has thrown her off balance. She hesitates, then replies she has no questions at the moment before inquiring about the next steps.

"As I'm sure you will understand," Lisa says, "we have a significant decision to make in choosing the right agent for our property. We'll be in touch by next week. Thank you for coming in and for showing interest in the listing."

She rises and shows Sarah to the door. As Sarah walks out of the building, she senses she's been hastily ushered out. Her prospects for a callback, she thinks, are not very good.

Now let's see how Emily does during the same process. On paper, she has the same qualifications as Sarah. In fact, her track record is identical to Sarah's.

Just as Sarah did, Emily receives a warm reception from Lisa in the lobby of the condo building. Lisa's smile is engaging, and with a confident handshake, she welcomes Emily before they start walking toward the condo. Throughout the brief walk across the building's common areas, past the concierge and the lounge, Emily and Lisa initiate a light conversation. "So how long have you owned this property?" Emily asks. "Did you have any trouble finding the building?" Lisa asks, followed by an offer: "Would you like a water or coffee before we get started?"

When they reach the condo, Lisa gestures for Emily to take a seat while she settles next to Mark. With a sincere smile and a quick review of Emily's track record, it's clear that Emily's experience speaks for itself. Lisa and Mark then delve into Emily's professional background, asking what fresh perspectives she could bring to marketing their property.

When Emily brings up a recent trend in luxury condo marketing she heard about, their interest is piqued, and they lean forward attentively, pressing her for details on her strategic approach. Sensing an opportunity to delve deeper, they wonder if Emily would be open to discussing her ideas about marketing their specific unit further. Emily agrees without hesitation. They continue the conversation, giving Emily the chance to display her ideas, insight, and proficiency directly.

An hour after Emily's arrival, Lisa notes regretfully that they must excuse themselves for another commitment but wonder if Emily is available to continue their conversation next week. Emily confirms her availability and expresses her appreciation for the engaging discussion.

Stepping out of the building, Emily feels a surge of confidence. She's established a meaningful rapport with both Lisa and Mark. And she feels optimistic about the next meeting she has scheduled for later in the week. For now, she has to hurry to the next meeting. It's with another high-profile client, a referral from a satisfied past client.

When Lisa and Mark discuss their impressions of the candidates that evening, Sarah's qualifications are considered first.

"No," says Lisa decisively. "She doesn't fit the bill. She lacked conviction. I can't picture her effectively marketing our property." Then Emily's profile comes up. "Very impressive," remarks Mark. "She has an energetic presence. I believe if we brought her on board, she'd be impactful right out of the gate."

Sarah and Emily. Two capable professionals with equivalent qualifications. Yet, in the eyes of Mark and Lisa, one seemed mismatched, the other distinguished.

If you were to ask Lisa and Mark about what made the difference, they might not directly say it was, for instance, the way they presented themselves that set one apart from the other—next to, of course, many other factors. However, in the real estate world, where a professional's identity can reflect an individual's meticulousness and diligence, this might have played a crucial role.

Even if she was dressed appropriately, it could have been Sarah's unadorned suit (lacking a hint of personal flair) or her conservative accessories (missing a spark of charisma) that didn't imprint upon Lisa and Mark the image of a dynamic, compelling force beneath an otherwise unremarkable exterior.

They may not acknowledge that their opinion of Sarah was formed from the moment they saw her in the building's lobby, dressed understated, leisurely seated, her posture a little too relaxed, her gaze idly locked on her smartphone, scarcely aware of the activity around her. Her apparent lack of engagement with her surroundings might have inadvertently suggested an absence of the readiness or drive that is highly prized in the fast-moving world of real estate.

The meeting? It might have been just an obligation. A formality. Sarah possibly never had a chance. As soon as they could, Lisa and Mark cut the meeting short and showed her the door. Despite Sarah's potential, she wasn't given a real chance.

In both real estate recruitment and client interactions, the instant perception of a candidate or agent is often an unspoken consideration. Although it may be regarded as trivial and not acknowledged as part of the formal evaluation process, it nonetheless plays a part in decision-making. Furthermore, legal and ethical standards prevent citing it as a reason for selection decisions. They can't and won't explicitly say, "We can't work with you because your external presentation doesn't align with our expectations." Such a statement would cross professional boundaries and could lead to significant repercussions.

They may also not acknowledge that they possibly already have formed an opinion about both agents before they even meet, influenced by the credentials and images presented in the online personas of the candidates. Nonetheless, the reality is that in any environment, the impression made by one's visual presence can subtly influence the final decision.

The principles illustrated in this story go well beyond just the client meeting setting. They are also highly relevant in your interactions with team members across a variety of leadership scenarios. It applies to presentations, team meetings, brokerage events, and any team-facing activity you engage in. Even in casual conversations or informal meetings, the impression you make shapes your team's overall view of your capabilities.

While your skills, knowledge, and deliverables are paramount, the subtle yet powerful cues of your presence frequently influence others' subconscious impressions of your expertise, diligence, and potential value. It shapes their openness to being influenced, guided, and ultimately led by you through the real estate journey.

A well-curated look of leadership sends a message of competence and dependability, establishing trust from the moment you step into a room. It's not just about looking good; it's about demonstrating respect for your role, the brokerage or agency you work for, and the people you serve. Each detail of your presentation speaks loudly and can be as pivotal to client confidence as the market insights or strategies you contribute.

Everyone knows the old saying "You can't judge a book by its cover." Yet the hard reality is that every day, in countless interactions, real estate leaders are judged by their "covers." It may not be fair, but it's an intrinsic human instinct. Although we encourage looking beyond the surface, there often isn't even enough time for others to form opinions based on deep observation. Remember, the exact amount of time—whether three or seven seconds—doesn't really matter. This brief window is not enough for people to thoroughly assess your capabilities or leadership qualities. That's why their brain defaults to the path of least resistance, the most straightforward route for gathering information—through their eyes. Humans are, after all, visual creatures.

Just imagine walking into a client meeting for the first time to present your marketing plan. In those initial moments until you get settled, you don't have much time to persuade them with facts and figures. Their first impression is dictated primarily by how you carry yourself and your overall presence.

Or think about joining a virtual property tour. Before you even begin speaking, the client has already subconsciously evaluated your appearance, body language, and facial expressions as well as the background behind you. Those visuals shape their perception before you can deliver your market insights.

Even when sending emails or posting social media messages about a property, any visual elements associated with your outreach contribute to whether a client sees you as someone credible and worth engaging with further. Your email signature, the fonts you use in your emails, any emojis you add, or the pictures on your profiles—each set the tone for your leadership identity.

Research led by Doug Vogel at the University of Arizona illuminated the speed at which our brains process images—60,000 times faster than text—and asserted that 90 percent of information is transmitted visually. Further emphasizing the predominance of visual information, Dr. Mary Potter from MIT led a study that found the human brain can process images seen for as little as thirteen milliseconds. This rapid processing suggests our brains are constantly and efficiently working to understand the visual world around us. These astounding facts highlight the immediate impact of visual cues on our perception, making your appearance a powerful communication tool.

Think about it, this means that before you've even spoken a word in a meeting, your visual presence has already conveyed a wealth of information about you. It's not just your clothing they subconsciously study; your body language, facial expressions, eye contact, gestures, and even the way you enter a room and carry yourself or the energy you project are all visual cues that communicate volumes.

Or perhaps you've experienced firsthand just how visually driven you are yourself. Have you ever spoken to a client on the phone and, based solely on their voice, formed a mental image of what they might look like? Then, upon meeting them in person, been completely surprised when they didn't match your vision?

At the meeting, Sarah might have believed her monochromatic look was neutral enough to be acceptable based on her past experiences. However, the moment Lisa observed her, her internal judgment was clear-cut. She might have subconsciously or consciously thought, "This candidate doesn't grasp the essence of our property's high-end image. And I don't have time to teach her."

Of course, it's absolutely possible that in a different market, for another property, Sarah's look or conduct would not have been a pivotal factor. However, for Lisa and Mark's standards and the particular property she sought to list, it was not a fit.

And your clients might think something similar: "This agent doesn't understand or align with our property's style. If they can't represent themselves properly, how can we trust them with our home?" They may consciously or subconsciously wonder if your lackluster professional identity is indicative of the kind of mediocre service they can expect when working with you. Fair or not, they may make assumptions that your outward presence directly correlates with your internal drive and expertise.

Whether when interacting with clients, team members, colleagues, or upper management, the split-second visual analysis of "does this person embody the qualities we're seeking?" can overrule other positive attributes you bring to the table. Your clients may dismiss you before fully appreciating the value you could provide, simply because the initial visual cues didn't instill the right level of confidence in you.

Just like we judge properties based on their curb appeal, wines on their labels, or movies on their trailers, clients judge real estate leaders through the lens of their own requirements and environments. The subtle cues of a leader's visual presence get filtered through the client's perceptions of what an ideal real estate agent should look and act like. A mismatch can lead to disqualification before dealing with your core competencies.

As for Emily, the moment Lisa saw her—even before they shook hands—she knew she was a contender. Her elegant outfit, the sleek style of her hair, her choice of eloquent accessories, her impeccable shoes—all were indicative of a woman who viewed herself as a real estate leader. And not just any leader, but one who could resonate with the dynamic spirit of the luxury condo market.

It might have been her creative flair in selecting clothes that broke the monotony, her unique way of marrying classic style with a modern twist, or her special knack for choosing accessories that hinted at a bold mind. We'll never know for certain. But something sparked in Lisa and Mark, a realization that she truly "gets it."

Yet, it wasn't vanity that dictated Emily's look. Far from being an overly glossy figurehead, her visual appearance stemmed from self-assurance. Her composed alertness set the stage. Standing tall and alert in the waiting area, she projected readiness and anticipation for the meeting.

When Lisa approached, Emily's smile was wide, authentic—a silent yet powerful introduction. She stepped forward, extending her hand first, ensuring a handshake that was confident and steady. Every micro-expression and gesture, from her steady eye contact to the assertive stance, communicated leadership. These subtle cues, frequently unnoticed, were the threads weaving a significant impression upon Lisa and Mark. Emily's outward presentation reflected her internal preparedness, a synchrony that they keenly observed. It was the finesse that transformed a prospect into a serious candidate.

Emily aimed to present as successful, but more critically, she wanted to be recognized as someone who could seamlessly integrate into the property's ethos. In fact, she hoped Lisa and Mark would see past her look and acknowledge her potential to contribute meaningfully. She aspired to render her appearance inconsequential—to be trusted immediately and seen as capable of excellence.

The Cost of a Poor Professional Identity

Perfection is unattainable, and everyone, including you, me, and even those in the highest echelons of the real estate field, is prone to missteps. Striving for flawless performance in every aspect of your professional identity is a noble goal, but it's important to recognize that occasional lapses are inevitable. Some errors may go unnoticed, but others could become widely known.

It could be a lapse in decorum at a brokerage gala, an inadvertently shared comment online that doesn't sit well publicly, or a day when your look might not meet the expected standards of your role. How you present yourself, how you dress, and how you carry yourself is constantly under scrutiny and can significantly influence perceptions. Not upholding the highest professional standards in every aspect of your work, including your visual presence, can result in significant consequences, such as the following:

- **Diminished credibility:** A real estate leader's visual presence plays a crucial role in shaping perceptions. If their professional identity does not align with expected standards, it can lead to doubts about their credibility and authority.

- **Loss of respect:** When real estate leaders do not consistently present themselves at their best, it can lead to a loss of respect from those around them. This diminished respect can affect interactions and dynamics within the team or with clients, impacting overall performance and cohesion.

- **Distraction from real estate objectives:** An inconsistent professional identity can divert attention from a real estate leader's strategic goals and hinder the primary focus on driving sales and market success.

- **Stagnant career trajectory:** A misalignment in professional identity can hinder a real estate leader's chances of landing more significant and influential listings and responsibilities.

- **Financial consequences:** A professional identity that is not in sync with market expectations can influence sales outcomes, directly affecting the brokerage's bottom line.

- **Diminished earning potential:** Perceived inconsistencies or errors in a real estate leader's professional identity can hinder their ability to secure listings and achieve bonuses or commissions, ultimately reducing their overall earning potential.

- **Undermining of professional boundaries:** Inappropriate elements of a professional identity can blur the lines of professional boundaries, increasing the risk of misinterpretation or misconduct.

- **Public image risks:** A lapse in professional identity can quickly become amplified in the media, social media, or other public spaces, damaging one's reputation and that of their brokerage.

You think this sounds far-fetched? Think again.

Yes, we all like to think about visual aspects as "superficial" factors, as something trivial or inconsequential. It's a topic many prefer to avoid or dismiss. Nevertheless, if we truly believed appearances don't matter—and weren't acutely aware of their consequences—why do so many of us still find ourselves posing some of these questions?

- Do I need to invest in luxury brands to create a successful professional identity?
- Is there a risk of going too far with luxury coming across as flashy?
- How casual is too casual for client meetings?
- Should I embrace a style that allows my personality to shine through?
- How much should I be influenced by my brokerage's branding and culture?

- Do I need to adapt my style depending on market, property type, or client demographics?
- Should I make an effort to appear younger and more relatable, or should I lean into a more mature, authoritarian look?
- Does it even matter when most of my interactions are virtual or on the phone?
- How can I avoid appearing disheveled after hours of property tours or open houses?
- For those casual "grab-a-drink" client meetings, where is the line between being relatable and too lax?

Have you ever caught yourself ruminating on any of these questions? You are not alone.

These are just a few of the underlying questions that cross many real estate leaders' minds, whether occasionally or on a regular basis, as they seek to balance the scales of authenticity and conformity within the bounds of industry norms. Each choice is like a thread in the tapestry of our professional identity, woven together in hopes of crafting a presence that resonates with both who we are and who we aspire to be in our careers.

Is there an easy answer to these questions?

You guessed it, there's no one-size-fits-all formula that can easily be applied for navigating this complexity, whether in person or online.

However, you might be surprised that my approach or recommendation is not to highlight your visual presence, but rather to neutralize it. Your goal should be to ensure your visual presence neither detracts nor defines you. Instead, you want the spotlight on your expertise, insights, and contributions. It's about mastering the art of subtlety—making sure your appearance is neither a talking point nor a distraction. Your aim should be that your presence—your eloquence, acumen, and ability—commands the room (or your social media feed), not what you're wearing.

Of course, you can instead also decide at any time to make your visual presence the center of attention. In fact, it's something I constantly embrace. If you've ever seen me on stage or watched footage from my engagements, you'll notice I step out in the most elaborate, unique looks—from striking colors to architectural cuts, from bold patterns to intricate designs, from avant-garde silhouettes to meticulously tailored ensembles.

For my engagements, I always aim to be the one who stands out, who draws eyes, who owns and captivates the room, even with my visual presence. But remember, I'm on stage—where all eyes are on me—and as a professional keynote speaker, my role is to captivate and engage my audience from the moment I step into the spotlight. And it's also my responsibility to not only deliver compelling content but to embody the principles of perception and visual presence that I advocate. I'm simply walking my talk, demonstrating firsthand the power of an intentionally crafted visual identity.

However, in your day-to-day leadership, this is an approach you must handle with care. You want to ensure your expertise, added value, and skills capture attention, making your visual presence an inconsequential backdrop rather than the focal point.

You should strive to be memorable for your performance, not your style. In the real estate arena, you want to let your achievements, insights, and leadership qualities shine, and your appearance should complement but not overshadow your true value.

And yes, while ideally your expertise should be the sole focus, the very nature of being in leadership demands an exceptional ability to shape positive perception through your professional identity at all times. Real estate leaders face unique challenges in this regard, encountering additional obstacles that those in non-leadership roles may not experience as intensely. These challenges include the following:

- **High-stakes encounters:** As a real estate leader, you have more frequent contact with high-net-worth clients who have higher expectations. Meeting these demands requires a polished professional identity and the ability to consistently deliver value under pressure.

- **Professional identity is your product:** If you work directly in real estate sales or a role that demands selling a physical property, your individual perception is your product. It is intrinsically tied to the perceived value of what you are offering—yourself and your brokerage's vision. The "packaging" you present matters immensely.

- **Constantly being evaluated:** You are perpetually being sized up by clients, team members, upper management, and stakeholders, all of whom are looking for any reason to disqualify you. Your visual presence is a continuous data point being scrutinized, in meetings, informal interactions, social events, and even when you are off work. Leadership presence doesn't take breaks; it's a 24/7 commitment.

- **Representing the brokerage:** As one of the faces of your brokerage, you are expected to embody the brand and its values at all times. This means you must consistently reflect your brokerage's mission and culture. Any deviation from this can impact not only your professional credibility but also the broader perception of your brokerage.

- **Overcoming preconceptions:** Let's face it, there might be professionals within or even outside your brokerage who think, "I could do this job just as well" (or maybe even think they could do it better). Hence, you must always strive to overcome any preexisting biases others may have simply based on your initial visible representation before getting opportunities to prove your capabilities.

- **Emotionally driven environments:** When it comes to their own personal real estate decisions, financial security, well-being, and significant property changes, clients tend to be more emotionally driven. These heightened emotions can profoundly influence their perceptions of and decisions about you.

- **Cultural differences:** Rarely do real estate leaders interact exclusively within a single cultural context. Their clients come from diverse cultural backgrounds, each with its own set of expectations. This diversity necessitates a nuanced understanding and adaptability to navigate through cross-cultural interactions.

- **Digital identity:** The landscape of leadership is rapidly changing with the continued development of the internet. Real estate leaders are now faced with the challenge of maintaining a digital identity that is under constant scrutiny. Every day, they engage in digital interactions, knowingly or unknowingly.

However, this complexity is an invitation, not a barrier. It is an invitation to lead with intentionality, to craft a narrative that transcends superficial judgments and taps into the deeper currents of human connection and influence. Your professional identity is not just a veneer; it's a conduit through which your true leadership essence flows.

And in the end, the true cost of a poor professional identity is not just measured in missed listings or failed commissions. It's in your lost potential to make a meaningful impact, to leave a legacy that reflects not just what you did, but how you made people feel. So as you move forward, let your professional identity be a reflection of the best version of yourself. Strive not for perfection, but for intention.

Shaping Your Narrative with Intention

Every choice you make, every action you take, and every impression you leave must be driven by a clear and purposeful intent. As a real estate leader, you cannot afford to leave your professional identity to chance. The stakes are too high, and the ripple effects too profound.

An intentional approach to your professional identity ensures you are not just reacting to the demands and expectations of those around you, but rather proactively shaping the narrative of who you are and what you stand for. It helps you strip away extraneousness and focus on what truly matters. This conscious effort is what sets great real estate leaders apart. It allows you to create a cohesive and compelling professional identity that resonates deeply with others, builds trust, and commands respect.

When your actions are driven by clear intentions, you are not just influencing others' perceptions on a surface level. You are more likely to inspire confidence and loyalty among your clients and team. This is because professionals are drawn to leaders who have a clear sense of direction.

So, it's essential to be intentional about how you present yourself in every interaction because this can have far-reaching effects. Whether you're engaging with clients, collaborating with team members, or representing your brokerage at industry events, your professional identity extends beyond the immediate interaction. It shapes perceptions, builds trust, and enhances credibility, not just for you but beyond you. Let's explore how your intentional identity reverberates across various aspects of your professional and personal life.

Consider the impact on yourself. When you, as a real estate leader, project confidence and competence through your professional identity, you're more likely to feel empowered and capable in your role. This self-assurance can translate directly into improved performance.

Reflect on your familial and social circles. The way you present yourself not only influences your own psyche, but also extends to the perceptions of your family members, friends, and broader social networks. Upholding a professional identity can establish a halo of trust and respect that permeates your entire personal support system.

Think about those you interact with. Clients, team members, upper management, business partners—all stakeholders form their initial impressions of you based on various factors, including your visual presence. By consciously presenting yourself in the best possible way, you inspire trust and credibility and lay the groundwork for stronger relationships and better outcomes.

Recognize the impact on your team's reputation. Your professional identity doesn't just reflect on you—it significantly influences your team's reputation as well. Team members aspire to confidently say, "I work for [Your Name]" as a badge of credibility and prestige. When you represent yourself with excellence, you not only gain their trust but also empower them to leverage your association to enhance their own standing in the brokerage and beyond, reinforcing their own professional identity.

Consider the ripple effect on your team members. As a leader, the way you present yourself sets the tone and example for your entire team. Your professional identity provides them with a model to emulate. You can inspire your team to raise their own professional standards and follow your lead.

Acknowledge the brokerage you represent. Whether operating within a corporate brokerage or spearheading your own real estate venture, the way you uphold high standards casts a reflection not just on yourself but on the brokerage(s) or brand(s) you're affiliated with.

Think about future employers and partners. The professional identity you build now can open doors for future career opportunities and strategic partnerships by preceding you with a respected, credible reputation before you even meet potential employers or business partners (or realize they are eying you.)

Reflect on the real estate profession as a whole. Beyond just your current role, the cumulative impact of real estate leaders upholding the highest levels of excellence elevates societal perceptions of the real estate profession overall. Your individual efforts contribute to greater respect and appreciation for the value that outstanding leadership provides.

Evaluate the industry-wide implications. Your individual leadership identity contributes to the collective perception of your industry as a whole. The way you present yourself sets a benchmark for professionalism and can influence public trust, client confidence, and the overall reputation of your field.

Generational impact and legacy. The example you set through your professional identity helps shape the next generation of real estate leaders. Your professional identity provides a benchmark for aspiring leaders to continuously raise the professional bar over time.

Without intention, your professional identity is subject to the whims of external perceptions and circumstances. You may find yourself constantly reacting to others' expectations and struggling to maintain control over how you are perceived. This reactive stance can create a disjointed and fragmented identity, making it difficult for others to understand who you are and what you stand for. In the absence of intention, your actions may seem erratic, your decisions may lack coherence, and your overall presence may come across as unstable. Others become unsure of what you truly stand for.

Your leadership loses its impact, your influence wanes, and your professional relationships suffer.

An unintentional professional identity not only confuses others but also undermines your own sense of purpose. It leaves you reactive rather than proactive. You become susceptible to the shifting perceptions and demands of others, losing control over how you are viewed and valued in your professional sphere.

Intention doesn't take a break; it cannot go on leave or take a vacation. It must be applied consistently, from the very first moment you interact with someone, throughout every single touchpoint, and even in the moments when no one is watching.

The Science of First Impressions

Let me introduce you to another study on first impressions that highlights the essential aspects of the research and its implications for our daily interactions. However, remember, this is just one piece of the larger scientific puzzle, illustrating that although first impressions can be powerful, their specific outcomes and interpretations may vary based on context and individual circumstances.

Neuroscientists at NYU and Harvard, led by Elizabeth Phelps, identified the brain systems involved in forming first impressions. Their findings, reported in *Nature Neuroscience*, show how we encode and evaluate social information to make initial judgments. The study was based on the idea that meeting someone new presents us with ambiguous and complex information, primarily visual but also involving other senses such as hearing, smell, and touch. We quickly process this information to decide if we're attracted to the person or not, a deeply ingrained process from our evolutionary past that helped our ancestors assess new people as friends or foes, leaders, or burdens. To understand this process, researchers designed an experiment examining brain activity during initial evaluations of fictional individuals.

Participants received written profiles of twenty individuals, each with different personality traits, and were shown pictures of these fictional people. The profiles included both positive traits (e.g., intelligent) and negative traits (e.g., lazy).

Participants then rated how much they liked or disliked each individual based on the profiles. For example, if a participant valued intelligence highly and was less bothered by laziness, they might form a positive impression. While participants made these evaluations, researchers used functional magnetic resonance imaging (fMRI) to observe brain activity.

The study revealed significant activity in two brain regions during impression formation. The posterior cingulate cortex, associated with economic decision-making and assigning value to rewards, and the amygdala, linked to emotional learning and social evaluations based on trust or race group, were both highly active. These areas were particularly engaged when encoding information that shaped the first impression.

The findings suggest that even with brief encounters and limited cues, our brains engage regions important in emotional learning and value representation. These regions sort information based on personal significance and summarize it into a single value—a first impression. Essentially, our emotional learning plus our values equals the leader's imprint.

Here's how the principles from the study apply to leadership:

First impressions set the tone: As a real estate leader, the first impression you make sets the stage for how others perceive your competence, trustworthiness, and overall effectiveness. Just as the study illustrated, your visual cues and even the briefest interactions can leave a lasting impression. It's essential to be mindful of these elements from the very first moment you engage with a client or team member.

Emotional and value-based perception: The study demonstrated that our brains use emotional learning and value-based assessment to form first impressions. For real estate leaders, this implies your professional identity is not just about the qualities you project, but also about how these qualities are interpreted by others. Your actions, expressions, and demeanor need to resonate with the values and emotional states of your clients and team.

The power of visual cues: The amygdala's role in processing visual information highlights the importance of visual cues in forming impressions. For real estate leaders, this means paying attention to the nonverbal elements of your professional identity, even before you speak.

Strategic use of first impressions: Real estate leaders can strategically use first impressions to their advantage. By consciously crafting your first impression to align with your and others' expectations and values, you can create an instantly powerful and persuasive presence.

Now, let's step away from the academic deep dive and move into something a bit more practical. Imagine this: I hand you a list of twenty random items to memorize. After a while, I ask you to recall them. Which ones do you think you're most likely to remember? If you're like most people, it's usually the first and the last items on the list that stick in your memory. Ever wondered why that is?

Let's take a peek inside your brain. Our brains are incredibly energy-efficient, made up of around 100 billion neurons. That's a lot of brain cells needing fuel to keep us ticking. Think of your brain like your smartphone or laptop. When the battery's running low, what happens? The screen dims, nonessential functions shut down, and the device goes into low-power mode to conserve energy until you can recharge it.

Now, let's bring this back to our initial list of items. Your brain, aiming to conserve energy, prioritizes what it processes and remembers. This is why the first and last items on a list—the ones your brain encounters first and last—are often remembered better. It's an efficient way to save energy while still holding onto critical pieces of information. Or, how often have you heard that when giving a presentation, the introduction and conclusion should be the most compelling parts? Same principle. Starting with a strong hook and ending with a powerful last statement ensures your message resonates long after you've finished speaking. Or, think of crafting an email, where we often spend more time perfecting the subject line or the opening sentence to grab the recipient's attention. And then there's the closing line that wraps everything up neatly. Again, it's the same principle at play.

So, what does this mean for your professional identity as a real estate leader? It underscores the importance of making a strong first impression and leaving a memorable lasting impression. The brain's tendency to remember the beginning and end more vividly than the middle means your initial interaction and your closing moments are crucial—or that at least it will flavor how everything in the middle is perceived. As real estate leaders, we need to harness this understanding to ensure the key messages and impressions we want to leave are clearly conveyed at the start and end of our interactions.

The Sustained Imprint

Make no mistake, don't think when I elaborate on first impressions that everything is dependent on those first micro-moments and the rest wouldn't matter. Your professional identity is deepened by much more—it's an ongoing process. Yes, your initial impression is pivotal, yet it's merely the precursor to what must become a deeply rooted perception. Consider this the inception of your "sustained imprint."

It's the ongoing cultivation of this first impression that cements your professional identity and maintains its potency over time. Without nurturing, even the most stellar beginnings can fade, losing their resonance and diminishing their initial influence.

I once developed and organized a leadership seminar for a group of real estate leaders from the organization I worked for in Europe. The participants were quite surprised to find out their trainer was not a person; instead, we trained them with the help of horses.

In one of the first exercises, we split the participants into two groups. The first group went into the riding area, where an unleashed horse was waiting for them.

The participants were told to walk in straight with confident steps, to appear strong, to keep eye contact with the horse, and to keep a straight face. When they arrived at the horse, they had to smack their horsewhips on the ground several times. The horse immediately began to run in a circle. The participants whipped and whipped, and they were briefed to stop when the horse appeared to be tired or simply ready for the next step to come.

When they put aside the whip, something rather magical happened: the horse followed them everywhere. Participants walked around the horse arena, and their assigned horse happily trotted after them. None of the participants had said one word to the horse. The horse just followed.

The second group received a different briefing. They were supposed to walk in and appear friendly and kind to the horse. They were told to motivate the horse by petting it, talking to it, and developing a relationship. They even brought in treats and encouraged the horse with all their hearts.

The first observation we made was that they had a really hard time making the horse run in a circle. It was obvious the horse wanted more treats and more tender loving care. Not much happened. The horse didn't follow and at one point didn't even come back for more treats because, obviously, there were no more.

What did we learn? Horses, much like humans, respond to the nonverbal cues of confidence and assertiveness. The first group's authoritative approach, conveyed through their posture, gaze, and decisive actions, left a compelling imprint on the horses, commanding respect and prompting a clear behavioral response.

This underscores the power of a strong initial imprint; without uttering a single word, their commanding conduct set the tone for the interaction, resulting in the horses' compliance and subsequent allegiance.

We also learned that being liked is not the ultimate goal of leadership; instead, being respected is. As a real estate leader, it's crucial to understand that respect is the foundation upon which effective leadership is built. Being liked is a bonus.

Now, this doesn't mean you should start wielding a metaphorical whip in your leadership style or with your team members and clients. Leadership is not about instilling fear or intimidation. It's about inspiring others through your actions and your unwavering commitment to excellence. It's about creating a culture of mutual respect, where everyone is encouraged to bring their best selves to the table and work toward a common goal. Leadership is not about force, it's about influence.

However, throughout the next days, we then also observed that the first group, emboldened by their initial success, celebrated with a sense of triumph, embodying the spirit of leadership and victory. And as time progressed, the complexity of their challenge unfolded. They began to display inconsistency in their conduct and actions.

To the horse, their once clear and commanding presence became unpredictable. And predictability, along with consistency, is the cornerstone of leadership—it's what engenders trust and respect. The first group, although initially successful in commanding attention, failed to uphold the robustness of that initial imprint. They did not succeed in cultivating it into a sustained imprint. The horses' diminishing responses was a clear testament to the group's faltering consistency.

The lesson was vivid and unequivocal: a leader's impact is measured not only by the strength of their initial imprint but also by the enduring presence they manage to sustain over time.

The game isn't over after seven (or however many) seconds. Outstanding real estate leaders leave lasting impressions by how they present themselves, always and everywhere—consistently.

Like Emily's experience, the positive imprint developed in mere seconds only got her in the door. It made the possibility of acceptance very real. It broke down the barrier between her and Lisa and Mark. However, the true test of her leadership and her professional identity will be in how she will sustain and build upon that initial approval, proving her value and substance in every subsequent interaction and decision in the near future and beyond.

Conversely, the negative impression that Sarah created caused the door to slam shut. It reduced the possibility of acceptance and created a barrier between her and the clients she met—who, in this case, had the power to either hire her or pass her by in favor of someone else. She will never even get the chance to prove her excellence or reveal the depth of her expertise because the brief encounter in the lobby had already casted a shadow on her meeting ahead.

In every setting that calls for your close attention, every interaction contributes to your lasting professional identity. This is true even during moments where you don't pay close attention because, truth be told, most of the day we run on autopilot, not recognizing that we are under constant observation.

I illustrate this in my keynotes by asking participants to take a selfie. As they excitedly prepare to capture their picture-perfect portrait, employing what digital culture has taught us—to position their face and body perfectly, to smile, to raise an eyebrow—I interrupt them with a seemingly impossible challenge: no posing, no adjusting their hair, no straightening their posture, no putting on their best "camera-ready" face. No tilting the head to find the most flattering angle, no sucking in the stomach or pushing out the chest, no last-minute adjustments to clothing or accessories.

Just a raw, unfiltered snapshot of their selves at that very moment. The result is a revelation: a picture that showcases how they are observed by others for most of the day—when they forget about their environment, when they forget they are always on stage, even when they think no one is watching. It's a stark contrast to the carefully curated images we often present to the world, a reminder that our true selves are not always the polished versions we'd like to portray.

This simple exercise is a powerful testament to the fact that our professional identity is not just crafted in the moments we are acutely aware of, but in the everyday instances when we let our guard down. It's in these unguarded moments that our real selves shine through, and it's these genuine glimpses that can leave the most lasting impressions on those around us.

The Invisible Filters of Perception

Put yourself into the shoes of a client, for just a moment. You find yourself ready to make one of the most significant financial decisions of your life—buying a new home. As you enter a real estate office, a sea of expectations and anxieties floods your mind. The receptionist is busy typing, not noticing you right away. As seconds tick by—which seem to feel like an eternity—you start to feel a bit ignored.

During that time, your eyes wander, and you can't help but notice the receptionist's nails look like they could use some attention. Their makeup and hair seem a bit much for such an early hour. When they finally do greet you, your patience has worn thin. You were on time, but now they've left you waiting. Finally, sitting down in the waiting room, you spot a crumpled piece of paper under a chair—missed by the cleaners, perhaps. The chairs around you show signs of age, with cracks and worn edges. Then, as you're called into the agent's office, a strange smell drifts from the staff room. Maybe they just had lunch?

The agent comes to get you, moving quickly, not stopping for introductions or handshakes. Their shoes have seen better days, and their suit has lost some of its crispness. All these little things add up in your mind, painting a picture of a place that might not be up to the mark. "No wonder," you think to yourself. "This seems to be the standard in this office"—a standard that feels lacking.

What you just experienced is the powerful influence of unconscious biases leading your mind. The sights and impressions, from the receptionist's appearance to the subtle cues of the environment, all funnel through your perceptions, coloring your expectations—possibly even without a word being spoken.

Unconscious biases are mental shortcuts or patterns of thinking that influence perceptions without conscious awareness. These biases often stem from deeply embedded social stereotypes, personal experiences, or prevailing cultural norms.

Let me share a personal anecdote that also illuminates how a variety of biases can work against us, even in the most intimate of settings. I am married to a German mathematician and engineer who works in finance and IT.

Now, let's indulge in a few stereotypes about Germans for a moment. On the one hand, in his life everything must be sorted and organized in a very particular way. He thrives on order and structure. My cultural background, on the other hand, is Mediterranean, which comes with a rather relaxed approach to life, embracing its fullness and finding joy in daily adventures that aren't always meticulously structured or planned.

Picture this: I'm the wife who goes to the refrigerator, takes out a bottle of sparkling water, and puts it back without securing the cap as tightly as my German husband would expect. Needless to say, it often leads to one of those minor household arguments that anyone living in a relationship is probably familiar with. But here's the interesting part—he finds every single item I leave open in our home, and I mean *everything*. But he never seems to register the things I do close, and believe me, I do close things.

What's at play here is also a medley of biases working against me. His brain embarks on a journey, subconsciously seeking proof and evidence to shape his perception of me in a particular way. He might think, "She's always leaving things open" or "She's not as organized as I am." But the reality is far more nuanced. It's not that I never close things; it's just that his mind is attuned to noticing the instances that confirm his preconceived notions.

The same is true for your clients and team members. Their minds go on journeys too, shaping their perceptions based on a complex interplay of preconceptions. They might fixate on a single interaction or characteristic that confirms their existing beliefs while overlooking the multitude of instances that contradict it.

As a real estate leader, recognizing and navigating these biases is crucial. It's not about striving for perfection or trying to control every perception. Rather, it's about understanding these biases exist and consistently presenting your best self in a way that invites others to see beyond their initial assumptions. It's about building a professional identity that, over time, paints a comprehensive picture of your leadership.

For you, those same unconscious biases could come into play when your clients or team members interact with you. Imagine a client arriving for a critical property viewing. If your car or attire appears disorganized, with papers strewn about and unkempt surfaces, this could unintentionally signal a lack of professionalism or preparedness on your part. Your client may start questioning your attention to detail before you even begin the property tour. Or if you greet them looking disheveled, their unconscious mind may jump to judgments about your ability to stay composed under pressure or properly represent their high standards.

The impactful takeaway is that we all innately make subconscious assessments that are further influenced by our unconscious biases. These biases are like silent storytellers, weaving narratives that may not necessarily be accurate or fair, shaping interactions and decisions in profound ways.

Confirmation bias, for example, is one of the most prominent unconscious biases. Confirmation bias is a psychological phenomenon in which individuals favor information that confirms their preexisting beliefs or hypotheses. It's the tendency to seek out information in a way that validates existing perceptions. This means we're more likely to notice details that support what we already think, often overlooking evidence to the contrary.

From the moment you walked through the door of the real estate office, your brain was picking up on cues and details that began to form an impression. When the receptionist didn't immediately look up, their unpolished appearance confirmed any lurking thoughts that the office is disorganized or unprofessional. Each subsequent observation, from the crumpled paper to the worn furniture to the agent's hurried entrance, built upon this initial judgment. Instead of seeing these as isolated instances, confirmation bias led you to interpret them as part of a pattern, reinforcing the belief that the office does not meet the standards of service you expect. Each detail seems to confirm your initial impression, and this bias can be particularly challenging to overcome once it takes root.

Anchoring bias is another pervasive mental shortcut we often take in which we rely too heavily on the first piece of information we receive—the anchor—and allow it to disproportionately influence our subsequent decisions. Once an anchor is set, other interpretations and information, even if more relevant or factual, tend to be viewed through the lens of this initial reference point.

Suppose the initial delay and the receptionist's disheveled appearance were the first bits of information you registered. These details likely became your anchor. As you continued to wait, even before noticing the crumpled paper or the smell from the staff room, your mind was already anchored to the notion that this office was subpar. This early anchor had an impact on your entire perception of the service provided, regardless of the actual quality of the real estate guidance you received.

The **horn effect** leads you to attribute negative characteristics based on a single perceived flaw, causing you to view all traits of an individual or entity negatively. For example, the receptionist's posture, which could be neutral or simply a product of a long day, might seem to you to indicate a lack of interest or enthusiasm. This bias can lead you to overlook any instances of competence or moments of kindness, focusing instead on the traits that seem to confirm your initial negative impression.

Negativity bias is another cognitive phenomenon in which negative aspects have a more significant impact on an individual's psychological state than do neutral or positive things. Essentially, we tend to pay more attention to negative experiences or information. Did you even notice the receptionist's meticulous uniform? Or what about the effort they put into carefully documenting client cases, a sign of thoroughness and dedication? Did you observe the efficiency with which they eventually handled your paperwork or the accuracy in their data entry? Similarly, the agent's speed may have been a reflection of their ability to manage a busy day effectively, ensuring every client receives timely service. However, these positive traits may have been eclipsed by the more immediate negative judgments, steering your overall impression toward the unfavorable due to negativity bias.

Selection bias will further force your mind to focus on every little flaw. You notice the tiniest speck of dirt, a slight tear in the curtain, or a faint noise from the air conditioner. You continue to selectively pick out all the negatives while ignoring anything positive about the experience.

Self-serving bias might come into play when you think, "I always pick the wrong real estate agent," making you feel even more justified in your negative assessment. This bias reinforces the idea that the problem lies within the office, not within any external factors or mere chance.

The **illusion of control** will make you feel like you could have avoided this bad experience if only you had chosen a different agent. You think you had control over the situation, and this misplaced belief adds to your frustration, making you believe you could have somehow foreseen and avoided the negative aspects.

And even after you've left the office, unconscious biases continue to steer your mind.

Availability bias, for example, ensures you overestimate the likelihood or importance of certain events or outcomes based on their ease of recall or availability in memory. This means the negative aspects you noticed loom larger in your memory than the positive ones. They become the ready examples that come to mind when you reflect on your visit or discuss it with others.

This tendency can extend to the point where you might find yourself at home browsing online reviews of the agent, unconsciously searching for further confirmation of your initial opinion. As you skim through numerous positive testimonials, they barely register; instead, your attention zeroes in on the few critical remarks. These resonate with your experience, reinforcing your perspective. Feeling validated, you consider it almost a duty to add your own critique to the mix.

Welcome to the **bandwagon effect** in action—a bias that compels us to adopt beliefs or behaviors because they seem popular or because others are doing it. In this context, the critical comments of others echo your own impressions, and the weight of collective criticism may feel like an undeniable proof, further solidifying your initial judgments.

The **Dunning–Kruger effect** may also take hold as you consider leaving a review. Feeling qualified to evaluate the entire real estate staff after a single visit, this bias overstates your own expertise, leading you to assert judgments that might not reflect the true caliber of the real estate professionals' skills and services.

The **sunk cost fallacy** may cause you to persist in viewing the office negatively because you've already invested time and energy in the visit, despite there being evidence of good service in the future.

I could go on and on. At the moment of writing this book, science is aware of approximately 185 biases that influence the human mind. These biases work beneath the surface of consciousness and affect every aspect of our lives, from the mundane to the critical, without us even realizing it. Understanding these biases is key to navigating the complex landscape of human thought and perception, allowing us to make more informed and deliberate choices.

And while unconscious biases can have a harmful and pervasive effect—manifesting in serious issues like housing discrimination and obstructing diversity efforts—they can also play a positive role for you in the brief window in which perceptions are formed. In this narrow but critical time frame, you can harness the power of these biases to your advantage.

By being aware of them and intentionally presenting yourself in a manner that aligns positively from the very first moments, you can influence others to see you in a more favorable light along the way. This doesn't mean manipulating perceptions dishonestly but rather ensuring the genuine and best aspects of your professional identity are what shine through and resonate the most.

For the real estate office we just visited, if, upon your arrival, the receptionist had briefly looked up and acknowledged you with a smile, making it clear they were wrapping up important work for another client's case, your impression might have been different.

Maybe they could have offered you a glass of water or a cup of coffee while you had to wait. Their unkempt nails maybe would have faded into the background, overshadowed by their meticulous uniform and the courtesy of their instant greeting. You might have thought to yourself, "They're really dedicated to each client's privacy and care."

As you took your seat, the receptionist's professionalism might have cast a positive light on the surroundings, making the waiting room's imperfections seem less significant; instead, you might have noticed the beautiful property photos on the wall. When the agent arrived promptly, their efficient manner could have been seen as a sign of a well-run office that values your time, turning a potentially negative first impression into a positive reflection of the office's standards.

Just as a client's perception of a real estate office can be swayed by subtle cues and unconscious biases, your professional identity is being shaped by a myriad of factors, many of which you may not even be aware of.

Consider a client walking into your office for a meeting. From the moment they step through the door, their mind is processing visual information and forming judgments. Is your workspace organized and tidy? Does your office reflect a modern, professional environment with up-to-date decor and branding that aligns with your brokerage's values? Are the materials and documents on your desk neatly arranged and professionally presented? Do you appear prepared and composed, reflecting a sense of confidence and readiness?

Each of these visual elements contributes to the client's overall impression of you as a real estate leader. As the meeting progresses, the client will continue to assess you based on a range of factors, from your appearance and body language to your communication style and expertise. Any perceived flaw, such as a lack of familiarity with recent market developments, inconsistent follow-up on prior communications, or even a slight hesitation when answering a question, can trigger the horn effect, causing the client to view your overall performance negatively.

Anchoring bias will ensure they cannot let go of that first initial impression, and selection bias will compel the client to continue to focus on every little flaw. They might notice if you frequently check your watch or phone during the meeting, if your technology runs into issues, or if there are typos in your materials.

These small details, while seemingly insignificant, can overshadow the positive aspects of your leadership if not managed properly.

Self-serving bias might come into play when the client thinks, "I always end up with these kinds of agents," making them feel even more justified in their negative assessment—even if you are doing your best.

The illusion of control will make the client feel like they could have avoided this experience if only they had chosen to work with a different agent. They think they had control over the situation, and this misplaced belief adds to their frustration, believing that they could have somehow foreseen and avoided these aspects.

The client's unconscious biases continue to shape their perception of you—making them believe along the way that they have a clear picture of you as a real estate leader and the professional identity you project.

By being aware of these biases, you can take proactive steps to ensure every aspect of your client's experience is positive.

But it's not just about avoiding negative impressions; it's about actively creating positive ones. In particular, by going above and beyond in your interactions with clients, you can harness the power of unconscious biases to work in your favor. This means you are using their unconscious biases to your advantage, which in turn means you are not just imprinting a good impression; it requires crafting an exceptional one. To stand out in a sea of sameness is about embodying excellence in every action and interaction and turning the ordinary into the extraordinary.

The question, then, isn't simply about being noticed—it demands being unforgettable. How can you truly stand out? The answer lies not just in what we do but in how we do it—with intention, with difference, with a touch of the remarkable in the everyday.

Standing Out for the Right Reasons

In the competitive landscape of modern real estate, where stakes are high and distinction is paramount, standing out is more than a personal goal—it's a professional necessity. Excellence is the new norm across the industry. Real estate leaders aiming to succeed must transcend the ordinary.

The truth is, "good" doesn't cut it anymore—"good" is the baseline, the expectation. To be perceived as a real estate leader—and to truly make an impact—you can't afford to simply fit the mold. Average blends in, and by blending in, you become invisible.

Think of the game Tetris for a moment. For some readers, Tetris is a nostalgic nod to the past, a digital relic from the days of clunky, handheld gaming devices. For others, perhaps of a younger generation, it's a classic that's been rediscovered on smartphones and modern gaming platforms. No matter the version you're familiar with, the metaphor stands: each piece that falls is designed to fit perfectly into a space, completing a line. The goal is to rotate and align falling blocks to complete lines.

But what happens when the line is completed? It disappears. This is a triumph in Tetris, but in your career, it's a warning. When you align too perfectly with the patterns already in play, you risk becoming part of the background—another completed line that serves its purpose and then vanishes into a sea of sameness.

When real estate leaders stand out, they do so by transcending the ordinary. They become the piece in Tetris that not only fits but also starts a reaction, changing the landscape, challenging the status quo, and bringing new possibilities into play.

Standing out means being the architect of your perception, crafting your professional identity with intention, and making choices that set the stage for how you're viewed in the real estate sphere and set you apart. It's about proactive distinction—carving out a space where your individuality and unique approach to your professional identity resonate unmistakably.

This requires being the memorable piece that doesn't just fill a gap but also creates a new path for others to follow.

You might be thinking, "Well, is it really always good to stand out?" For a pop star, standing out from the crowd in any way they can always bring positive returns. Whatever gets their name mentioned in the press will help sell their records. For an entertainer, standing out from the crowd, regardless of the reason, is also good to an extent. If they get on the evening news simply because everybody thinks they have done something out of order, they've won the game. Or think of my example for a moment again—as the one being on stage or working an audience, it's crucial to stand out to captivate and engage effectively.

But in the real estate universe, standing out for its own sake is a terrible idea. In the real estate space, there's a good way to stand out and a bad way to stand out.

The surest path to standing out in the best way is to consistently do three things:

- **First, be your very best self,** bringing your unique personality to the forefront and cultivating a professional identity that highlights your individuality.

- **Second, embody and uphold the highest values of your brokerage and the industry,** serving as a living testament to its mission and principles and ensuring your professional identity reflects the integrity and values your brokerage and the real estate industry stand for.

- **And third, don't just meet expectations—surpass them,** striving to surpass them by going above and beyond what's anticipated and developing a professional identity that is synonymous with excellence.

The bad way to stand out is . . . well, any other way.

Imagine once again walking into that real estate office. You're greeted not just by a friendly receptionist but also by a wave of innovation. The receptionist, with a welcoming nod, directs you to an interactive kiosk. It's an engaging check-in experience where you can personalize your visit. In the waiting area, you're immersed in an environment designed for comfort and education. You instantly notice a refreshment bar—a gesture of hospitality. Here, the receptionist offers a selection of herbal teas and nutritious snacks, transforming the waiting time into a moment of relaxation and nourishment for the body and mind.

In your hands, a tablet becomes a window to new knowledge. With an augmented reality application, you explore property topics in a way that's interactive, immersive, and personalized to your real estate journey. Posters on the wall spring to life, providing a depth of understanding that pamphlets could never match. Amidst this, a subtle scent fills the air. The receptionist explains it's aromatherapy, intentionally chosen to create an atmosphere of calmness. It's a thoughtful touch that eases the inherent tension of waiting for a significant financial discussion. Instead of outdated magazines, the area features an exhibition of local artists' works. The space is transformed into a sanctuary that indulges your senses and promotes a serene environment.

At every turn, this office has gone above and beyond. Even feedback is revolutionized. With a real-time device, you can express your level of satisfaction, empowering you as a partner in the service experience. Later in the day, the agent even personally calls to check in, instead of delegating this task to administrative staff or a piece of software. This office has redefined what it means to stand out, ensuring that from the moment you walk in to the last farewell, your experience is anything but average.

As a real estate leader, you too must reimagine what it means to stand out with your visual presence and "look of leadership." Your visual presence is a powerful tool that can enhance your professional identity and create memorable connections with your team and clients, or it can undermine your credibility and diminish the respect you command if not managed with intention.

But standing out as a real estate leader isn't about making grand, exuberant changes. It's about the many small details that collectively create a powerful professional identity. It's not about being the loudest or most flamboyant; it's about being the most refined, consistent, and impactful.

When Details Speak Loudest

In a world brimming with competence (and competition alike), where "good" has become the standard, the nuances of excellence whisper the secrets of distinction. The fine print and subtleties can amplify your professional identity in a symphony of sameness, because paying attention to detail speaks volumes.

It's the crisp dress shirt or the perfectly tailored suit that projects authority, the signature accessory that hints at creativity, or the elegantly simple briefcase that showcases one's work with sophistication. It's the polished shoes, subtly gleaming from beneath a conference table, that hint at a refined and thoughtful choice. It's the well-kept notebook with its neatly aligned edges, whispering of your methodical approach to your work. It's the gentle click of a quality pen, the unspoken ally of your thoughts during client meetings, and the smartwatch that discreetly keeps you on schedule. It's the unique business card that reflects a personal identity or the thoughtful office decor that signals innovation. It's the photograph on your or your brokerage's website that captures you engaged in a dynamic team discussion that sends a powerful message of collaboration. Or it's the professional headshot on your LinkedIn profile that speaks volumes about how seriously you take your role.

Your professional identity is like a puzzle, each piece playing a crucial role in creating a complete and cohesive narrative. Every detail is a vital part of the whole. When every piece is thoughtfully placed, you build a powerful and memorable professional identity. Yet just as a puzzle with missing pieces feels incomplete, neglecting any aspect of your professional identity can leave your narrative fragmented and less impactful.

In this puzzle, no piece is too small or insignificant. Instead, these nuances collectively weave the narrative of a real estate leader's commitment to their field and their inherent role as a trailblazer.

In my keynotes, I often illustrate how small details can significantly influence judgments by sharing a fascinating video based on an actual study. The research involves twins who are dressed identically for various professional settings, such as two police officers, two managers, or two doctors. They sit side by side, looking completely alike in every way, with one crucial difference: one of them is chewing gum.

Participants are seated in front of the twins and asked a series of questions, "Which of them would be more likely to give you a parking ticket?" or "Which of them would be more inclined to give you a raise, or even fire you if you asked for one?" The questions delve deeper into the twins' perceived social lives, with participants speculating about which twin gets invited to more parties or has more friends, both real and imaginary. Even their supposed sex lives come under scrutiny.

Surprisingly (or perhaps not), most individuals favor the gum-chewing twin across all these scenarios. The presence of that small, seemingly insignificant detail—the act of chewing gum—is enough to sway perceptions and create an entirely different narrative around each twin.

Of course, in reality, the relationship between a minor detail and these various outcomes is not so simple or clear-cut. Nevertheless, the study, which was later used in an advertisement video for a chewing gum brand, provides a compelling illustration of how easily our perceptions can be influenced by minor, often irrelevant factors.

As real estate leaders, it serves as a powerful reminder of the need to be mindful and in control of the subtle details that can shape others' perceptions of us, sometimes in ways we might not anticipate or intend. It underscores the importance of being intentional about every aspect of our professional identity.

In the same vein, it's the finer details of presentation that can also sometimes cause real estate leaders to stand out—and be remembered—for less favorable reasons, be it the overly casual hairstyle that might be perceived as too laid back for a client meeting; a palette of colors more befitting of a fashion runway than a real estate setting; the jewelry that clinks and clatters distractingly during property tours; a bold fashion statement that might overshadow the substance of a listing presentation; a shirt buttoned improperly that can seem careless; an overpowering cologne; or a laptop covered in an array of personal stickers, which could undermine the organized professional identity one aims to project in a client meeting. All these details, however small, could overshadow expertise and intent and inadvertently shift the focus away from a real estate leader's professional contributions.

It's these memorable yet incongruent details that could lead someone to recall an individual not for their real estate acumen but for their sartorial choices, thinking, "Ah, yes, that's the agent with the rainbow-colored hair." Or "Sure, I remember those neon glasses, but I actually don't recall their name."

Such details, however small and even irrelevant, have the potential to cast a long shadow, sometimes causing the positive aspects of an interaction to fade from memory.

Is this fair? Certainly not. However, humans are built to think this way—this includes you, and it includes me.

Let's turn to another experience in a medical practice. Decades ago, I found myself in need of a physical therapist to treat my back pain. Back then, when the internet was still a distant dream, I recall the quaint process of selecting a practitioner based solely on insurance coverage and luck of the draw in a paper telephone directory.

Yes, I know—this certainly dates me, as some readers might not even remember a time before Google.

At my appointment, I stumbled into a place that felt more like someone's home than a clinic. I navigated through a cluttered living room adorned with an eclectic assortment of plants, art, and odd collections—a creative chaos, to say the least. Finally, I arrived at the treatment room, painted in sterile mint green, housing a physical therapy treatment table enveloped in disposable paper.

Right there on this paper, which I thought was there for hygienic reasons, my eyes swiftly caught an unexpected sight: the remnants of a chicken bone. You read that right: the remains of what once was supposedly a chicken wing. Despite my initial shock—and I wish I could say I left instantly—I found myself discreetly disposing of the evidence in the therapist's trash can. Moments later, the therapist entered with a friendly greeting, apologizing briefly for his absence due to a quick lunch break he took between patients.

I don't remember much about the treatment itself. To be fair, it might have been wonderful, his medical analysis might have been on point, and his treatment plan might have made sense. He might have shown genuine concern for my condition, offered insightful advice, and demonstrated remarkable skill. Perhaps he had even gone above and beyond, providing a tailored exercise regime or following up with a call to check on my progress. I don't remember how much I paid or how convenient the location might have been. All that lingers is the image of that chicken bone.

And did I ever return? The answer is no.

Have you ever walked into a client's home and instantly noticed a strange smell that made you question how easy it would be to sell the property? Or perhaps you've entered a kitchen only to see a sink full of dirty dishes, and you immediately started to doubt the client's commitment to maintaining the home for showings. Maybe you've sat down in a living room, where the sight of scattered toys and overflowing laundry baskets made you think about the extra effort required to stage the home properly.

These initial impressions can quickly shape our expectations and strategies for selling the property.

Think back to the real estate trainer at a seminar whose brilliant insights were momentarily overshadowed by the typos in their slide deck. Or the appraiser who arrived at a property inspection late and disheveled, leading you to instantly question their professionalism and reliability. Perhaps you recall the home inspector whose thoroughness was doubted the moment you noticed their tools were haphazardly organized, suggesting a lack of attention to detail. Or the stager whose expertise was put into question when you saw their own car, cluttered with personal belongings, parked outside the listing.

The bottom line is that one incongruent visual detail can distract from the core value you offer, even if just for a split second. But in the world of leadership, one second of doubt is an eternity that others will seize upon.

Successful real estate leaders understand and accept that everything is rooted in the details. Those little details can make us stand out for reasons both right and wrong. Although some of these details may seem trivial at first glance, they possess great power. This is because in the world of leadership, where many professionals are deemed average, it's these subtle nuances that allow you to stand out—for all the right reasons. In a sea of sameness, where many leaders blend into the background, these details become your secret weapons.

Embrace the power of nuance and use it to your advantage. And always remember, it's not about perfection; it's about intention. It's about making a conscious effort to present your best self in every interaction, no matter how small.

Chapter 2
Your Professional Identity

The Indelible Mark
Etched in Others' Minds.

Chapter 2: Your Professional Identity

Let's begin with some clarity on the lingo. Terms abound in this context. Some might refer to it as "executive presence" or "professional image," others might use "professional persona," and there are those who speak of "personal branding." Each term, although distinct, converges on a core principle: the essence of how you present, position, and define yourself.

I choose to call it "professional identity" because it encompasses more than just the surface level of your professional life. Unlike "executive presence" or "professional image," which can imply a focus on outward appearance, "professional identity" digs deeper. It is the integration of your values, skills, experiences, and personal traits into a cohesive whole that defines who you are as a professional—and not just your look. It's a holistic approach that considers every facet of your professional existence, from your appearance and behavior to your communication, digital footprint, and the environment you create around you. It's this comprehensive nature that makes "professional identity" the most fitting term to describe the multifaceted and deeply personal nature of how we navigate our professional lives.

Our professional identity is a direct reflection of the attention and care we invest in our most valuable asset: ourselves. Each detail is a thread in the fabric of the impression we weave, not only benefitting our self-image but also enhancing the esteem of the organizations we represent.

This is because the reputation of any real estate organization—whether it's, for example, a corporate brokerage, independent agency, property management firm, or mortgage company—is significantly influenced by the professional identities of its representatives.

And this is particularly true for real estate leaders. As the direct link between the brokerage and its clients, they are often the first point of contact and play a crucial role in shaping client perceptions. Their professional identity can either reinforce the brokerage's credibility or undermine it, making their conduct pivotal in establishing and maintaining a positive reputation.

Although the story of Sarah and Emily unfolded in a luxury condo setting, the essence of the so-called seven-second rule is universal. Whether you're stepping into a high-stakes client meeting, engaging in a virtual property tour, posting market updates on social media, presenting a listing proposal, or attending a real estate networking event, your professional identity is established almost instantly. Changing this first impression once it's formed is notoriously difficult, and altering it can be an uphill battle. As you already know, once formed, it becomes a filter through which all subsequent interactions are assessed.

For example, when Lisa and Mark initially encountered Sarah and unconsciously placed her in the "not suitable" category, changing that snap judgment was nearly impossible. Because the said snap judgment is rooted in Lisa and Mark's cognitive framework, it subconsciously forced them to seek out information that reinforced their initial perception while ignoring evidence to the contrary. Her chance to make a positive impact was lost before it truly began.

On the flip side, when Lisa and Mark met Emily, her professional presentation immediately pegged her as credible and competent. Instantly, she became a strong contender for the listing. Lisa and Mark's swift categorization was governed by the same cognitive processes that shaped their earlier judgment.

Subconsciously, their brains were now compelled to confirm their initial favorable impression, scanning for evidence to support Emily's suitability. In this subtle dance of cognition, their brains worked diligently, albeit unknowingly, to validate that Emily was indeed the exemplary choice for the listing.

This is the power of your initial imprint and its impact on your professional identity. It is the ambition of every real estate leader to be seen instantly as competent and capable, maximizing every opportunity to exhibit their leadership potential.

Your professional identity is a narrative, a story told from multiple perspectives: one that you tell yourself, one that others tell you to your face, and most importantly, one that others tell behind your back.

Like every story, it has a starting point. Think of it as the cover of a book that intrigues you. Once you've decided to buy into the cover and purchase the book, you turn page by page, further reinforcing whether your decision was worth it. It might be so boring you give up after the first few chapters, or so exciting you can't wait to get to the last page, or even better, leave you hoping there will be another book added to the series.

Similarly, your professional identity starts with the initial impression—the cover. If this cover is compelling, people will delve deeper, seeking to understand the full narrative. Every interaction, every decision, and every element is a new page in this book. If the story is engaging and compelling, people will want to keep reading. They will look forward to every new chapter, reinforcing their positive perceptions and anticipating more from you. On the contrary, if the initial pages are disappointing, they might not continue reading, and your opportunity to influence and lead effectively may be lost.

Professional identity is about creating a story that others want to be a part of, a narrative that they trust and believe in. So, just like an intriguing book cover and a captivating story, your professional identity should draw people in, keep them engaged, and leave them eagerly anticipating the next chapter.

And once again, we need to realize that a book is often purchased based on its visual appeal. Surely the title matters, maybe the author's name or a recommendation can sway our choice, but even then, when we find ourselves scrolling through online bookstores, it's the books with a striking cover that instantly stand out or reinforce what the title, author, and recommendation promise.

These critical moments of visual assessment can happen in any real estate setting, and such encounters could unfold in numerous settings. Instead of the described client meeting situation, Sarah might have been a mortgage broker discussing a financing strategy, or Emily could have been a property manager pitching her services. The context may vary, but the specific situation matters less than the universal truth: within those first crucial moments, based on their self-presentation, they are categorized as "doubtful" or "promising."

And wouldn't you rather be the one with the exceptional book cover for your narrative—the one that instantly stands out without having to say a word (or in this case, write one)? Wouldn't you want to be the one with a cover that catches the eye, intrigues the mind, and leaves a lasting impression even before the first page is turned? The one that clearly invested in a professional book designer rather than just downloading an average template?

Just as a book cover can captivate a potential reader, your professional identity should captivate those around you. This is not about superficiality; it's about presenting the best version of yourself. Your visual presentation serves as the cover of your professional identity. It's what draws others in and encourages them to look deeper, to turn the pages, and to invest in the narrative you have to tell.

So why settle for anything less than an extraordinary cover? Why not invest in every detail of your presentation, ensuring it aligns with the values and strengths you wish to project?

And just think about it for a moment: What impact would this intentional choice have on yourself?

Realizing you are not a forgotten, dust-covered book left behind on a shelf or an overlooked title in an online listing. But let's be real—you've already answered these questions for yourself. After all, you picked up this book, recognizing the importance of this topic for yourself, and here you are, still engaged and turning pages.

So, it will come as no surprise that your look of leadership shapes not only how you're perceived by others but also how you perceive yourself. Looking the part can significantly enhance your confidence and effectiveness. The visual choices we make can act as a form of self-expression, offering a visual language that communicates our identity, mood, and confidence level—not just to others but also to ourselves. When a real estate leader puts on clothes that align with their role and that they feel good in, it can create a positive feedback loop: they may feel more assertive, confident, and in control, which can, in turn, elevate their performance and the quality of their client and team interactions.

For many real estate leaders, the right outfit serves as armor against the world, providing a sense of preparedness for whatever the day may bring. There's a reason why terms like "power dressing" have emerged; clothing can be empowering.

Research by Hajo Adam and Adam D. Galinsky from Northwestern University has shown that when you dress in a way you perceive as powerful, you can experience psychological changes that include increased abstract thinking, which is a key component of leadership and strategic thought.

This intersection of clothing and psychology is known as "enclothed cognition," which describes the impact that clothes have on the wearer's psychological processes. Enclothed cognition is a powerful testament to how the external—the clothes we choose and the professional identity we present—intersects with the internal, shaping how we see ourselves and, in turn, how we are perceived as real estate leaders.

But is it really just about our clothing? Is our visual presence truly the sole driver of either our self-perception or how others perceive us?

Clearly, it's not the sole factor, yet it's quite significant. Our visual presence acts as a critical filter through which all our professional behaviors and communications are perceived. It's a silent but powerful language that precedes and punctuates every action.

There's a famous study by Albert Mehrabian that suggests the words you say—the actual words, not the tone or inflection—account for only 7 percent of the imprint you make. It's called the 7 percent–38 percent–55 percent rule. Words account for 7 percent, tone of voice accounts for 38 percent, and body language accounts for 55 percent of the imprint you make.

One might think (or might have heard) this study suggests it's not important what you say or how you behave; it's only about appearance. Of course, that's just not true. It's another internet myth, and Mehrabian himself made countless attempts to clarify that the study should not be interpreted this way.

Still, countless coaches, trainers, and speakers use this study to suggest the thing that matters most is how you appear, neglecting the significance of verbal communication and behavior—and that is just not true.

However, if you have only a few seconds to make a first impression, your visual presence takes on greater importance. No one is exempt from this instinctive process; it is a fundamental aspect of our human cognition.

You'll recall that Sarah and Emily had identical track records. (This is not just a hypothetical; in today's competitive real estate market, among dozens of qualified agents for a given listing, there are bound to be several candidates who look the same on paper.) The chances are good that when Lisa and Mark first met them and they had a conversation—that is, during the first few seconds—there wasn't much difference in the actual words they spoke.

Those initial moments are simply too fleeting to demonstrate one's verbal competence. Instead, in such brief encounters, it's our visual and perhaps even our sensed presence that speaks volumes. Remember, the human brain, in its quest for instant understanding, relies primarily on the visual cues it receives, complemented by the subtle undercurrents of what it feels rather than what it hears.

As Sarah and Emily awaited their turns in the lobby, silent narratives unfolded within mere moments of Lisa's approach. They casted a long and sometimes indelible shadow, setting a stage where unseen forces came into play. These forces, subtly yet powerfully, influenced the trajectory of Lisa and Mark's judgments. Like invisible threads, they pulled at the fabric of perception, weaving assumptions and conclusions based on the initial visual encounter. These energies, silent but potent, elevated Emily in a halo of positive light and shrouded Sarah in a cloud of skepticism.

When I speak at an event, I usually demonstrate this by entering the stage and saying nothing. It's a long, uncomfortable silence that envelops the room, one that I create purposefully to ensure my audience members scrutinize only my visual presence. Then I start counting out loud to seven, demonstrating how fleeting this time frame is.

It's the first time they hear my voice, register my accent, and gauge my tone. It's the opening page in the narrative I'll write on stage, following the cover they've already judged. I confront them with a plethora of decisions they already made about me without knowing anything about my background, skills, knowledge, or the value I bring to the event at this point. And it's highly likely that dozens of audience members will approach me afterward and say something along the lines of, "How did you know? What magic or witchcraft did you apply to read our minds?"

The reality is much simpler. It's a combination of the wardrobe choice I intentionally made on this day, the audience I researched beforehand, and the insights of years of my own research or those of others (such as, once again, Dr. Solomon's study).

And even if the way this research has been described on the internet cannot be taken at face value, what it clarifies is which elements and thoughts of the eleven factors become more relevant depending on the situation you are in.

For example, in a client meeting situation, such as the one Sarah and Emily experienced with Lisa and Mark, critical attributes such as competence, honesty, believability, credibility, and trustworthiness are paramount.

Now, imagine you are instead in a dating situation. Here, different elements come into play. Your level of success and confidence may be under a bigger spotlight, as potential partners gauge your suitability based on different criteria than in a professional setting.

While the eleven elements remain consistent, their weightings shift based on the observer's motives.

So, how can you reinforce the elements that are crucial? How can you better highlight and ensure the focus remains on what matters? By using the tools you already have. No, this book isn't about discovering some hidden secret or acquiring new things. You already possess everything you need in your repertoire; it's simply a matter of applying these tools more intentionally.

The ABCDEs of Your Professional Identity

Your professional identity encompasses a multifaceted blend of choices you make—both small and large—that shape how you're perceived and valued in your role. And this professional identity is the sum total of your choices in the following five areas:

- appearance;
- behavior;
- communication;
- digital footprint; and
- environment.

Here's an easy way to remember these five key elements: just think "ABCDE."

APPEARANCE: Your appearance is your first opportunity to make a statement without saying a word. It's the canvas upon which your personality is painted and the initial impression you leave on others. From the moment someone lays eyes on you, they're subconsciously processing a wealth of information about who you are and what you represent.

Let's start with your body image—the first thing others notice about you. Whether you're tall or short, slim or sturdy, these physical attributes shape the initial perception others form. But it's not just about the shape or size of your body; your overall health, both physical and mental, also radiates through your appearance. A vibrant glow of vitality or a worn-down facade can speak volumes about you.

Clothing is your armor in the battlefield of first impressions. The fit, brand, style, quality, patterns, and colors of your clothes silently communicate your taste, personality, and attention to detail.

Accessories are the finishing touches that add flair to your ensemble. Whether it's a statement watch, a sleek tie, or a pair of polished shoes, these embellishments speak volumes about your personality and style.

Maintaining your wardrobe is an often-overlooked aspect of personal presentation. Well-kept garments demonstrate your commitment to professionalism and, again, attention to detail.

Your personal grooming is the final touch that completes your appearance. Skin care, hair care, dental hygiene, and nail maintenance all contribute to your overall presentation.

Your appearance is a silent language that speaks volumes about who you are and how you approach life—and your real estate career. It allows you to set the stage for meaningful connections and interactions. It is not just about looking good; it's about embodying the values and confidence you want to project.

When you appear with intention, you send a powerful message to the world that you are ready to lead and make an impact.

BEHAVIOR: At the core of your behavior lies your attitude—the vibrant colors that illuminate your outlook on life, ranging from sunny optimism to somber clouds of negativity. Your attitude not only sets the tone for your interactions but also serves as a compass guiding you through your career's twists and turns.

Adding depth to your behavior is your charisma (or lack thereof), drawing others into your orbit with your irresistible charm. That magnetic force most of us wish to have.

Navigating this rich tapestry of behavior requires emotional intelligence—the wisdom to read between the lines and steer gracefully through the intricate labyrinth of human interaction.

But no masterpiece is complete without a sturdy foundation of ethics and morals, the bedrock upon which your character stands firm.

And as you navigate the vast canvas of human interaction, diplomacy and courtesy are hopefully your guiding stars.

Your behavior is the brushstroke that adds depth and dimension to your professional identity. It's the unwavering commitment to integrity, empathy, and respect that sets you apart. In every interaction, let your actions reflect the real estate leader you aspire to be, because it is through consistent, intentional behavior that you build a legacy of trust and influence.

COMMUNICATION: The most important part of communication doesn't include any words. Instead, at the heart of communication lies active listening—the art of truly tuning in to others. Through active listening, you not only hear the words spoken but also understand the emotions and intentions behind them.

Adding depth to your communication are your body language and facial expressions, the nonverbal and silent-yet-eloquent language of gestures, postures, and movements.

Your body and face speak volumes, conveying emotions and attitudes that words alone cannot capture.

And what melody is complete without your voice—the instrument you play every single day? Your voice, with its range of tones, pitches, and cadences. From the gentle lilt of persuasion to the commanding resonance of authority, each vocal element adds depth and richness to your message.

Words themselves are the very essence of communication, and your language palette is the paintbrush with which you craft your message.

Yet it's not just what you say but how you say it that shapes the narrative of your communication. Your communication habits, whether empathetic and concise or passive and manipulative, set the tone for your interactions, guiding the flow of every conversation and shaping the dynamics of relationships. Your accent or dialect may add richness and diversity to these conversations.

Finally, your written communication is the ink that flows through the veins of our interconnected world.

Communication is the lifeblood of your professional identity. It's not just about the words you choose, but the authenticity and passion behind them. Effective communication bridges gaps, builds trust, and fosters collaboration. Every conversation is an opportunity to reinforce your professional identity, so speak with clarity, listen with empathy, and engage with purpose.

DIGITAL FOOTPRINT: Your digital footprint is like a breadcrumb trail scattered across the internet, with each crumb leaving its mark on your online reputation. From intentional actions to those unwittingly left behind, each interaction shapes not only your digital presence in the first step, but also your offline persona as a consequence.

At the heart of this trail lies email communication, a digital handshake that speaks volumes about your professionalism and reliability. Similarly, your mobile communication offers glimpses into your accessibility and efficiency.

Venturing into social media, with your posts, comments, likes, and shares, can enhance your online reputation, positioning you as a credible and insightful voice within your digital real estate community.

In virtual meetings, your digital footprint takes on a new dimension, showcasing your adaptability and professionalism in remote settings.

Meanwhile, chats and forums serve as arenas for digital discourse, where your contributions reflect your expertise, engagement, credibility, and influence within online real estate communities.

The frequency, savviness, and authenticity of your digital interactions shape your unintentional footprint, influencing how you're perceived in the digital realm.

Your digital footprint is the modern extension of your professional identity. In an age where online presence is pivotal, your digital actions and interactions can amplify your credibility or undermine it. Be mindful of the digital legacy you create—every post, comment, and message contributes to the narrative of who you are as a real estate leader. Curate your digital footprint with the same care and intention as your physical presence.

ENVIRONMENT: Your environment isn't just where you are—it's the vibrant backdrop against which your professional journey unfolds, filled with both tangible and intangible elements that shape your daily experiences and leave an indelible mark.

Your network, for example, isn't just a list of contacts; it's a living ecosystem that provides support, fosters collaboration, and unlocks doors of opportunity at every turn.

Then there's the spaces you inhabit—the places where you live, work, and everything in between. They're more than just physical locations; they're sanctuaries of productivity, creativity, and inspiration.

And let's not forget about the journey itself—the daily commute, the occasional getaway, and the leisure pursuits that recharge your batteries.

From the thrill of exploration to the tranquility of downtime, these experiences add color to the canvas of your professional life, infusing it with excitement, balance, and rejuvenation.

Your environment isn't just a backdrop; it's a character in the story of your professional journey, shaping the plot and influencing the outcomes at every twist and turn. So take a moment to look around. What do you see? How does it make you feel? And most importantly, how can you optimize it to support your goals, reflect your values, and lead you toward success and fulfillment?

Your professional identity is a mosaic of countless pieces, each one carefully chosen and placed to create a masterpiece that is uniquely you. From your appearance to your behavior, communications, digital footprint, and environment, every element plays a vital role in shaping how you're perceived and valued as a real estate leader. Each piece of this mosaic works together to create a comprehensive and compelling professional identity.

And, yes, while an impeccable look can open doors, it is your behavior and communication that will sustain those connections. Simply looking great is insufficient; your actions and words must consistently support the professional identity created by your appearance. Genuine engagement, ethical behavior, and effective communication are what build trust and long-lasting relationships.

In today's digital age, your digital footprint holds immense relevance, often serving as the first impression clients and partners encounter. This initial online presence can determine whether you will have the opportunity to engage in meaningful in-person interactions. Your online activity, therefore, must be managed with the same intentionality as your physical presence.

Lastly, the environment you cultivate is a critical, yet often underestimated, aspect of your professional identity.

While it is widely acknowledged that surrounding yourself with the right individuals is crucial, many of us continue to associate with people who neither enhance our professional identity nor contribute positively to our self-perception. Creating an environment that supports your goals, reflects your values, and encourages growth is essential for sustaining a strong professional identity.

Each piece of this mosaic works together, and consistency across all of these elements is what transforms a collection of good impressions into a powerful, lasting narrative. Because in the end, it's not just about making a strong first impression; it's about consistently living up to that impression, day in and day out, that truly defines your professional identity.

Internal and External Consistency

Consistency is the backbone of any credible professional identity. The key is to ensure your appearance, behavior, communication, digital footprint, and environment all sing the same tune. You can't present yourself as reliable and trustworthy in your clothing, but then behave unpredictably or unprofessionally during interactions. You can't curate a digital presence that conflicts with who you are in the real estate world. Surrounding yourself with luxury and glamour while aspiring to a reputation of humility and service sends mixed messages. Exhibiting professional conduct during business hours but behaving recklessly or inappropriately outside of work leads to confusion. Using a professional tone in verbal communication but having written communications full of errors or lacking clarity undermines your perceived competence.

Only when all elements of your professional identity align harmoniously does the message of who you are and what you stand for become unmistakable, compelling, and memorable.

This consistency also extends beyond your personal presentation to maintaining a coherent professional identity both within your brokerage and in the wider real estate world.

- **Your internal professional identity** pertains to how you present yourself, behave, and communicate within the intricate ecosystem of your brokerage. This encompasses interactions within your team and department, collaborative projects with cross-functional teams, or consultations with colleagues or upper management. Real estate leaders who demonstrate unwavering consistency in their professional identity within their internal sphere earn the respect and trust of others within their brokerage. Think about the ripple effect of your actions: how your commitment to excellence can inspire your team, enhance collaboration, and drive overall brokerage success. Reflect on how every decision, every interaction, and every presentation contributes to the larger narrative of your leadership within your brokerage.

- **Your external professional identity,** in contrast, pertains to how you represent yourself and your brokerage to external stakeholders. Each public interaction—whether it's a listing presentation, a networking event, a speaking engagement at an industry conference, a meeting with a client, or an engagement within your community—is a stage upon which your professional identity is showcased. The perceptions you create in these moments extend beyond your personal reputation; they influence how your brokerage and its leadership are viewed in the broader real estate market. Imagine the power you have as you craft your brokerage's reputation, because each of your interactions is a testament to your dedication to professionalism and your strategic acumen in navigating the complexities of the real estate business.

As a real estate leader, however, this principle, while seemingly straightforward, encompasses a complex and nuanced challenge that extends beyond your individual effort.

This is because the true test of a real estate leader's capability lies in ensuring this consistency permeates the entire team. The challenge is not only to maintain one's own standards but also to inspire and enforce these standards across all team members. When the entire team adheres to agreed-upon norms, it fosters unity and professionalism, creating a cohesive and credible front that significantly enhances the brokerage's image. Conversely, any deviation by team members can lead to confusion, undermining team cohesion, the brokerage's reputation, and, ultimately, your professional identity as a leader.

It's essential for your team to understand their appearance, behavior, communication, digital presence, and environment inside and outside of their respective brokerages also reflect on you and the brokerages they represent. And although many team members may diligently adhere to protocols and standards within the brokerage, there can be a tendency for some to inadvertently overlook these standards outside of professional settings.

At any given time, your team members may encounter clients, partners, or community members outside the brokerage setting. It's crucial they also maintain the highest level of excellence in these interactions—anytime, anywhere, and with anyone upholding the reputation of the brokerage they are affiliated with.

Picture this: You're at a major real estate conference, representing your brokerage. You've spent months preparing for this event, honing your pitch, and perfecting your presentation. You step onto the stage, and all eyes are on you. In that moment, your appearance, your behavior, your communication—everything about you—is a reflection of your brokerage. Now imagine that, in the audience, there's a member of your team. They're not presenting, but they're still representing your brokerage. And let's say, hypothetically, that this team member has chosen to attend the conference in clothing that's more suited for a casual night out than a professional event. Or maybe they're engaged in behavior that's less than professional—speaking loudly during presentations or failing to show respect to other attendees.

In this scenario, the inconsistency between your professional presentation and your team member's actions creates a discordance that can undermine your credibility as a leader and the reputation of your brokerage. Even though you're presenting yourself in a professional manner, the actions of your team member can cast a shadow over the entire brokerage.

Or picture this: One of your team members brings everything to the table you wish for in in-person meetings. Every day they show up as the picture-perfect real estate professional, displaying impeccable behavior and communication. Yet, one day you encounter their social media posts filled with unprofessional or controversial content. This inconsistency can severely impact your reputation as a leader and the brokerage's reputation because it suggests a lack of oversight or a disconnection between professional and personal standards.

Only when everyone is on the same page, presenting a united front of excellence, will the overall image of your brokerage be strengthened. When there are inconsistencies, this creates cracks and sends mixed messages about what you and your brokerage stand for, which can lead to confusion and mistrust among clients and stakeholders.

Maintaining internal and external consistency is not solely the responsibility of real estate leaders; it extends to every team member. If this resonates with you as a familiar challenge, another chapter of this book will delve deeper into strategies and techniques for effectively addressing these challenges with your team, providing tips and insights to support you in having these sensitive conversations.

In today's interconnected world, you and your team are under constant observation. There's unlikely much to hide, as every action, interaction, and presentation can be scrutinized both within and outside of your brokerage.

Your professional identity thrives on visibility—what would it matter if it were perfect but no one notices it? It's not just about crafting a flawless professional persona; it's about ensuring it's seen and recognized. You need to amplify your visibility and trust that those you lead can step into the spotlight with you, enhancing the collective brilliance of your team and brokerage.

From Shadows to the Spotlight

A picture-perfect professional identity that remains hidden in the shadows serves no one. Hence, in one of my other books, *Discover Your Fair Advantage*, I dive extensively into the different visibility levels that exist for real estate leaders within the workplace. If you haven't picked up a copy yet, I wholeheartedly invite you to do so—your professional library will thank you, and so will your real estate career—it's like a professional supercharge!

But for now, let's revisit these visibility levels quickly and explore what they mean for your professional identity. As we journey through these levels, you might just find yourself recognizing where you currently stand and where you aspire to be. So, let's see where you fit in the visibility spectrum.

Visibility Level 1: Being Invisible

Some real estate leaders operate under the radar, their efforts going unnoticed despite their significance. They might blend into the background, performing critical tasks without recognition from upper management. These leaders remain largely unknown, their contributions hidden behind a veil of anonymity. This invisibility can stem from a lack of confidence, insufficient skills to stand out, or inexperience in navigating the competitive real estate landscape. Some may even choose this path consciously, seeking to avoid unwanted attention, additional responsibilities, or the pitfalls of office politics. However, for others, this invisibility is not a choice but a circumstance they struggle to change.

Their potential remains untapped, waiting for an opportunity that might never come. This level makes upper management ask, "Who is this person, and what do they do?"

At this level, your professional identity is faint, almost indistinguishable, and lacks the clarity needed to be recognized and valued. Your appearance may seem nondescript, blending in with the crowd. Your behavior might come across as passive, failing to draw attention. Your communication may be limited or unnoticed, with few recognizing your voice or input. Your digital footprint could be minimal and your environment may be unremarkable, blending in with its surroundings and lacking distinctiveness.

Visibility Level 2: Being Common

Achieving a basic level of visibility as a real estate leader means being recognized for your consistent performance. You are known for doing a good job, but there's nothing that really sets you apart from others. You become a reliable, yet common presence in the brokerage, acknowledged for your contributions but not seen as a unique asset. Upper management may recognize your name and associate you with competence, yet they do not perceive you as someone who can add exceptional value in new or challenging roles. You are seen as dependable but interchangeable. This common visibility makes upper management think, "They do a pretty good job, but what else?"

At this level, your professional identity is stable yet unremarkable, blending into the background without making a distinctive impact. Your appearance may seem professional yet typical, lacking any standout elements. Your behavior might be seen as competent but routine, without showcasing unique strengths. Your communication may be clear and functional, but not particularly memorable or influential. Your digital footprint could be consistent but unremarkable, reflecting a standard presence without distinction, and your environment might be generic.

Visibility Level 3: Being Unique

At this level, you have moved beyond mere competence as a real estate leader and have started to demonstrate unique capabilities and assets. You stand out among your colleagues and are recognized for specific strengths that add unique value to your role and brokerage. This visibility is not easily achieved; it requires self-awareness, confidence, and dedication to highlight what makes you unique. You are known for doing exceptional work in a way that is distinctively yours. Upper management begins to identify you as a valuable resource, considering you for opportunities that require the specific attributes you consistently showcase. This visibility level prompts upper management to say, "This real estate leader is an outstanding performer with a unique approach that benefits our brokerage."

At this level, your professional identity is clear, distinctive, and marked by specific strengths that set you apart from others. Your appearance may be distinguished by unique elements that reflect your professional identity. Your behavior might be characterized by a proactive approach that sets you apart. Your communication may be impactful and memorable, clearly conveying your unique perspective and value. Your digital footprint could be strategic and engaging, showcasing your expertise and thought leadership in real estate. Your environment might be thoughtfully curated to reflect your standards.

Visibility Level 4: Being Referrable

At the highest level of visibility, your unique strengths and capabilities are not only recognized but also advocated by others. You are referred and recommended for opportunities without your direct involvement. Your reputation precedes you, and upper management discusses your potential in high-level meetings, often considering you for promotions or new roles because of your well-known and unique assets. This level of visibility ensures you are seen as an irreplaceable asset to the brokerage, and it significantly enhances your real estate career trajectory.

Upper management is likely to say, "Have you heard about this real estate leader? They're incredible and perfect for this new opportunity."

At this level, your professional identity is robust, influential, and continuously promoted by others, making you a sought-after real estate leader within and outside your brokerage. Your appearance may exude a commanding presence that is instantly recognizable and respected. Your behavior might be seen as exemplary, consistently demonstrating leadership qualities that inspire and motivate others. Your communication may be highly influential, with your words carrying significant weight and impact. Your digital footprint could be extensive and authoritative, positioning you as a go-to expert in real estate. Your environment might be a reflection of your high standards and success, reinforcing your professional identity through its exceptional quality and attention to detail.

Did you find yourself in one of these levels? Ultimately, visibility level 1 (being invisible) will prove to be quite detrimental to your leadership career. Even visibility level 2 (being common) prevents you from being noticed. When your visibility stagnates at these levels, you might often think to yourself, "Everybody knows that I am doing good work, so why am I not getting ahead?"

And I know how that feels. I was stuck in visibility level 2 for many years during my corporate career. I was a hard worker, deeply committed to the success of my brokerage and its upper management, and I received plenty of recognition from my leaders for my outstanding results and work ethic. They knew they could count on me for any task, and I was involved in a variety of different projects. Yet, when opportunities arose, my name was never mentioned, even though I knew exactly what I was capable of offering and had the necessary assets. Nowadays, I understand it isn't enough to simply be known for being good at something. There are many leaders out there just like you and me—hardworking and reliable.

In my journey from visibility level 2 to higher levels, I had to intentionally work on every aspect of my professional identity. This transformation began with a deliberate focus on my appearance. I reevaluated my wardrobe choices and my look to ensure it reflected the leadership status I wanted to project. I turned my attention to my behavior and forced myself to become more proactive in meetings, sharing my insights confidently and ensuring my contributions were noticed. I refined my communication skills, both verbal and written, ensuring they were clear, concise, and impactful. I strategically curated my online presence, ensuring my social media profiles and professional networks reflected my expertise and achievements. This involved proactively creating content that showcased my knowledge and engaging with others in my field. And, I paid closer attention to my environment. I surrounded myself with individuals who supported my growth and challenged me to excel, and needless to say, I had to let go of many others.

Through these intentional efforts, I transformed my professional identity from being common to being unique and referable. This holistic approach ensured that every facet of my professional identity worked in harmony, allowing me to stand out.

The key to reaching visibility levels 3 (being unique) or 4 (being referrable) is to stand out from the crowd and be instantly and consistently visible to upper management within your brokerage and the real estate industry. Only this visibility will bring attention to what you do, how you do it—and most importantly—who is doing it: you!

Your goal is not just to craft an exceptional professional identity; you need to ensure it's noticed, recognized, and remembered. The more refined and intentional this identity is, the easier it is to achieve. This requires relentless self-awareness, strategic visibility, and a steadfast foundation of confidence in yourself.

Chapter 3
Leaders Look Confident

Confidence Isn't Thinking You Are Better. It's Realizing You Have No Reason to Compare Yourself.

Chapter 3: Leaders Look Confident

Imagine a skyscraper—a marvel of modern engineering, reaching toward the sky with its gleaming windows and impressive facade. But what keeps this towering structure standing strong, day after day, year after year? It's the foundation—the unseen, unsung hero that lies beneath the surface, providing the stability and strength that allows the building to rise above the rest. Sure, the design, materials, and craftsmanship all play crucial roles too, but it all starts with a solid foundation. Without it, even the most impressive architectural feats would be destined to crumble. Just like a skyscraper, a real estate leader's success is built upon a foundation too—but not one made of concrete and steel. No, the foundation of a real estate leader is built on confidence. It's the bedrock upon which their professional identity is constructed, the invisible architecture that supports their every move.

So, what exactly is confidence? What does it mean to look confident, and why would it even matter for a real estate leader? Well, it's not as simple as it seems. You see, confidence isn't just about having a firm belief in your own abilities or the decisions you make. It's much more than that. It's also about having an aura of competence, empathy, and unwavering authority that inspires trust, respect, and a sense of security in everyone around you—whether it's your upper management, team members, clients, or the wider community.

In the high-stakes arena of leadership, few qualities are more essential than an unwavering sense of confidence. This inner belief in one's abilities to adapt, persist, and ultimately succeed is a prerequisite for thriving amidst the constant rejections and uncertainties inherent to the profession.

Research has explored this vital link between confidence and leadership performance time and again. Studies by Robert S. Heiser at the University of Maine and David McArthur at Utah Valley University affirm that confidence and enthusiasm have long been recognized as prerequisites for exceptional leadership. Their findings suggest the most successful leaders exude an air of confidence that allows them to remain adaptive and resilient in their approaches. Similarly, a research paper by Guangping Wang at Louisiana State University indicates leaders with higher levels of confidence tend to outperform their less confident counterparts. An inner reserve of belief empowers them to invest greater effort, even when facing repeated setbacks and naysayers.

However, confidence, the cornerstone of your professional identity, often finds itself besieged by a multitude of enemies. These adversaries, lurking in the shadows, can chip away at even the most self-assured real estate leader's confidence. Let's explore some of these saboteurs and how they might impact you.

Comparison: The Thief of Joy and Confidence. It's so easy and quite common to fall into a cycle of continuously comparing yourself to others. You might find yourself constantly measuring your performance, achievements, and even your own worth against your colleagues. It's a subtle process that can chip away at your confidence and leave you feeling inadequate. Imagine this: you're achieving great things, but you can't help glancing at that leaderboard, comparing your commission figures to the top performer. Every time you compare your quarterly sales to someone else's, it's like a small piece of your confidence erodes. It's a common tendency, but it's crucial to recognize that comparison is the thief of joy and confidence. True confidence comes from within.

It's about celebrating your unique journey, your strengths, and your successes. It's about building a sense of self-worth that can withstand the pressure to measure up.

Rejection: The Constant Companion of Leadership. Rejection is an ever-present challenge—like the uninvited guest to the leadership party. As a real estate leader, you face a constant stream of "no's" as part of your daily work life. Every rejected offer, unanswered call, and lost listing can feel like a personal setback, slowly wearing down your confidence. However, rejection is part of the real estate territory. But true confidence lies in turning those "no's" into opportunities for growth. It's about understanding that every rejection brings you one step closer to a "yes" and, luckily, far away from a "maybe." And most importantly, it's about having the resilience to keep pushing forward, no matter how many obstacles you face.

Imposter Syndrome: The Inner Critic. Do you sometimes hear that nagging voice in your head that whispers, "You're a fraud," even when you're succeeding? The higher you climb up the leadership ladder, the louder that voice can become. You might start questioning whether you truly deserve your success, wondering if it's all just luck. In the real estate world, where success is constantly measured and celebrated, imposter syndrome can be particularly challenging to overcome. The key is to own your achievements, reminding yourself that your success is the result of your hard work, talent, and determination. You belong exactly where you are.

Quota and Pipeline Pressure: The Weight of Expectation. In leadership, the pressure to meet and exceed expectations can be relentless. You're constantly under scrutiny, with your performance metrics, sales forecasts, and revenue targets all being closely monitored. The weight of expectation from upper management and your team can be substantial.

When you miss a target or your pipeline is looking lean, it's easy to start doubting yourself. But true confidence comes from focusing on the process, not just the end result. It's about trusting in your ability to adapt, innovate, and lead your team through challenging times. It's about maintaining a steadfast belief in yourself and your team, even when faced with setbacks.

The Rapid Pace of Change: Staying Ahead of the Curve. The real estate landscape is constantly evolving. New technologies, changing client expectations, and market shifts can make it challenging to stay confident in the face of rapid change. You might worry about becoming obsolete or not being able to keep up with the latest developments. But true confidence is about embracing change. It's about committing to continuous learning, being willing to experiment and adapt, and believing in your ability to navigate uncharted territory. It's about leaning into the discomfort of the unknown and trusting in your resilience and adaptability.

Confidence is a complex concept, built from a combination of internal and external factors. While the psychological battle against these enemies is ongoing, there is one powerful weapon in a real estate leader's arsenal that can help to shield against these confidence saboteurs: your visual presence.

At first glance, the link between your look of leadership and confidence might seem superficial, like it's just about "dressing the part." But the impact of your external presentation on your internal confidence is far more significant than you might think. With all the challenges and self-doubts real estate leaders face, a powerful look of leadership can serve as a suit of armor, a tangible reminder of your professionalism, competence, and readiness to lead—for yourself and others.

Let's first explore the internal dimension of dressing with confidence.

Dress for the confidence you want, not the insecurities you have. It's a universally acknowledged truth that when we look good, we feel good. This isn't shallow vanity, but a reflection of how closely intertwined our self-esteem and self-perception are with our external appearance. Clothes do more than just cover us up; they can make us feel good or uneasy, especially at work. Researcher Kim K. P. Johnson and her team, in their article "Dress, Body and Self: Research on the Social Psychology of Dress," found that when professionals dressed appropriately for their job, they felt more confident. They associated psychological discomfort with wearing inappropriate clothing to work. Mary Katherine Brock's research confirms young professionals' confidence is heavily influenced by the clothes they wear. Even color seems to matter, as Craig Roberts and his research team point out, because certain colors, such as red, could boost confidence in individuals.

Or, you might remember the research I mentioned earlier by Hajo Adam and Adam D. Galinsky, who introduced the concept of enclothed cognition, which means what we wear can change the way we think and feel. Their study focused on the significance of wearing certain attire in the real estate field and how this attire impacts mental processes. They discovered that wearing attire associated with expertise and success can sharpen a person's focus and carefulness. However, the effect varied based on the described purpose of the attire: clothing labeled as belonging to successful real estate agents enhanced attentiveness more than those described as everyday wear. This indicates that the influence of clothing on cognitive function depends on both the symbolic association and the physical act of wearing the garment.

The armor of a well-considered wardrobe serves not just as a physical outfit but also as a psychological bolster. What we decide to put on every day can shape how we feel about ourselves and how we interact with others.

Just think about it for a moment. How often have you felt a dip in confidence because of a poorly chosen outfit? Have you ever cringed when a client mentioned they found your social media profile, knowing you have an outdated profile picture? Have you ever walked into an important client meeting only to realize your shirt has an obvious stain? Or found your confidence wavering due to unkempt hair or a rushed shave? Have you noticed how a cluttered background visible on a virtual meeting detracted from the professional identity you aimed to project?

By taking the time to create a look of leadership that exudes capability, authority, and self-assurance, you're not just influencing how others see you; you're engaging in a powerful act of self-affirmation. You're telling yourself that you are worthy of investment, that you are prepared to face the challenges of the day, and that you are capable of handling whatever comes your way.

Now let's take a look at the flipside, the external dimension.

Dress with intention and style and then inspire with substance. From others' point of view, a real estate leader exuding confidence through their visual presence subconsciously garners more attention. Their presence instantly captivates, signaling expertise worth listening to. You've likely experienced those kinds of leaders who walk into a room and fill the atmosphere with an undeniable aura of authority and charisma. It's as if their very presence commands respect and admiration. They carry themselves with a certain poise, a self-assuredness that's unmistakable. Their posture is upright, their movements purposeful, and their gaze direct and engaging. It's not just about what they wear, but how they wear it.

When you encounter such leaders, you can't help but wonder, where does this magnetic presence come from? What's the secret behind their unwavering self-assurance? And then, as if to answer your unspoken questions, they begin to speak. Their words are articulate, their insights profound, and their vision compelling. They have the substance to back up their style, proving that their confidence is not just a facade, but rather a reflection of their true capabilities.

This is the power of a leader who understands the importance of both the visual and the substantive aspects of leadership. They know their appearance is the first point of contact, the initial impression that sets the tone for all subsequent interactions. But they also recognize their appearance is just the beginning—it's their real estate expertise, their decision-making skills, and their ability to inspire and motivate others that truly sets them apart.

When you take pride in your visual presence and couple it with genuine substance, you create an empowering culture of achievement. Your team members look up to you not just because you look the part, but because you embody the values and vision of the brokerage. You lead by example, demonstrating that success is not just about looking good, but about being good—good at what you do, good to your team, and good for the brokerage.

Dress to spread confidence like a wildfire. Confidence is contagious, especially when it emanates from someone in a leadership position. The confident aura you cultivate and the intentionality behind your refined visual presence radiates outward, affecting your entire team's psyche and performance.

When you carry yourself with confidence, it instills in your team members a sense of pride in who they work for and who they represent. They might begin emulating the high standards you embody, feeling inspired to show up as their best selves. Your confidence becomes their confidence.

And this ripple effect can extend far beyond your immediate team. It can permeate the entire brokerage, shaping its culture and reputation. When you consistently demonstrate confidence through your visual presence, it sends a powerful message to all stakeholders, which communicates stability, competence, and a commitment to excellence that inspires trust and respect.

Conversely, any glimpses of insecurity or half-hearted efforts toward your own professional identity can breed uncertainty amongst all ranks. If you seem uninspired in your presence, it gives permission for your team to make excuses as well.

As the old adage goes, "they will never care how much you know until they know how much you care." The contagious effect of a real estate leader's confidence is perhaps the most pivotal force for elevating everyone's performance.

So, as we explore the "look of leadership" in the pages to come, let's approach visual appearance not as a superficial consideration, but rather as a potent tool in the confidence-building arsenal.

Leaders Are Confident about Their Body

Imagine a world where the tiniest creatures perform the mightiest feats. Think about ants for a moment. Despite their miniature size and weight, ants achieve extraordinary things. They forge complex tunnels, transport massive loads, and collaborate with remarkable efficiency. This incredible strength and resilience, packed into such a small creature, show us that size and weight do not determine capability or value. Instead, it's about leveraging what you have to its fullest potential

So, let's start off our discussion about confidence by setting aside the things you can buy at a department store or online and focus on the most important suit. The one you were born with: your body. Recognizing the body as a fundamental aspect of your identity and a vessel through which you offer leadership is the first step toward deeper self-confidence. You need to acknowledge your unique body characteristics—your strengths and your limitations—and embrace them as integral parts of who you are.

Because who hasn't, at least once in their lifetime, wrangled with thoughts like, "I'll never be taken seriously because I'm too short," "How can I lead if I can't even manage my own weight?" "I'm too tall and people find me intimidating," or "I look so underweight; I don't appear strong enough to be in charge." It's natural—most of us have been there. And it will come as no surprise to you that these self-destructive thoughts can undermine your confidence.

But the truth is, your physical attributes do not define your leadership potential. Instead, it's about leveraging what you have to its fullest potential, just like those tiny ants achieving extraordinary feats despite their size.

And truth be told, although there certainly are some tricks when it comes to dressing your body, you'll never be able to fully change the fundamentals: someone short will never be tall; someone overweight will never look skinny. This acceptance is not resignation but a celebration of diversity and your individuality.

Nevertheless, let's explore how weight and height impact perceptions of leadership and confidence.

Confidence beyond the scale: Weight is often perceived as a reflection of personal discipline and lifestyle. In various professional spheres, particularly those with a focus on health, fitness, or overall well-being, weight can indeed influence perceptions of credibility and authority. Consider, for example, industries such as personal training, health care, or nutrition, where professionals often serve as role models for healthful living. In these fields, the expectation is that your visual presence aligns with professional advice. Similarly, leadership roles that demand a high degree of discipline and self-control might also scrutinize physical fitness as a proxy for these traits; think of dealing with high-end luxury properties, where a fit appearance might be seen as a reflection of the attention to detail and high standards clients expect. The connotation being if they can't maintain high standards for themselves, how can they deliver it for coveted clientele? There are indeed professional areas where real estate leaders are more expected to personify the ideals, values, and lifestyle aspirations underlying the properties they represent.

When we talk about weight insecurities, our minds often instantly zero in on the overweight, but that's just half the story. Bias related to weight manifests in two opposing but equally damaging stereotypes: those who are heavier may be perceived as lacking self-control, whereas those who are thinner may face misjudgments of being too delicate to manage the stress and responsibilities of leadership positions. Both of these stereotypes are unjust and overlook the individual's actual capabilities and contributions.

The same is true for research—most studies related to weight and bias in the workplace also focus predominantly on the overweight perspective, often neglecting the challenges faced by those who are underweight.

For example, research by Patricia V. Roehling and her team highlights how obesity affects perceptions of promotability, demonstrating that obese candidates are often seen as less suitable for promotions compared to individuals with other physical conditions. This bias also extends to leadership perceptions, where obese individuals are significantly underrepresented in top positions within major real estate firms. Additionally, studies by T. L. Brink, which are further supported by Eden B. King, reveal that obesity can heavily influence views of one's leadership abilities.

A study by Joseph A. Bellizzi and Ronald W. Hasty uncovered that leaders broadly viewed obese professionals as less suited for challenging, client-facing territories that demand constant engagement and presence. Interestingly, the discriminatory effects were lessened for roles involving minimal face-to-face client interactions, such as telephone positions. Perhaps most disconcertingly, the research indicated that obese professionals faced harsher disciplinary actions from their leaders when accused of ethical breaches or misconduct incidents.

However, despite the impact of weight on professional perceptions as highlighted by various studies, the most crucial factor is your own relationship with your body weight because it significantly influences your confidence. This internal perception of self-worth and assurance should be strong enough to override external biases and shape how you're viewed. Hence, if you are seeking to align your weight with your health goals and professional identity, the options include the following:

Carry your weight with poise and confidence, no matter the number on the scale. You are who you are in the body you currently have, and it's no one else's business why you are in this body. It could be related to health issues, your eating habits, your lifestyle choices, or even genetics.

Keep in mind, however, that the right fit of clothing can significantly affect how your weight is perceived by yourself and others. Ill-fitting clothes can add pounds or create an unflattering silhouette that distracts and often backfires. Conversely, well-tailored clothes can enhance your look of leadership, contributing positively to your confidence and overall perception. The key is a strategic selection of clothing that fits impeccably, thus avoiding adding unnecessary bulk or implying a lack of attention to detail—both of which can detract from your professional identity.

And ignore any outdated and oversimplified methods of categorizing body shapes. You are more than an "apple" or a "pear"—you are a real estate leader, a professional, a force, and an individual whose worth is defined by accomplishments and abilities, not by the contours of a silhouette. Your shape does not confine your potential; it is your presence, your expertise, and your actions that carve out the real shape of your influence and impact.

This advice, although once popular, not only pigeonholes you but also often overlooks the nuances and individuality of each person's personal style. It disregards the fact that whereas some individuals may wish to downplay their "pear" shape, others may want to embrace and accentuate it with pride. No one-size-fits-all concept can dictate whether you should highlight or downplay your shape. Your body, your rules—your style should be a reflection of you, not a fruit comparison chart.

Opt to lose or gain weight with a focus on health rather than solely on aesthetics. Yes, let's rip off that band-aid—there's no middle way, no easy getaway, no shortcut. If you feel your weight, no matter which end of the spectrum it's on (too heavy or too light), impacts the way you perceive yourself or the way others perceive your professional identity, you might need to apply disciplined, consistent, and consequent measures.

Positive changes in weight can lead to a boost in confidence and enhance your overall perception as a real estate leader. Yet, as you probably know, this process should be undertaken with health as the priority, ensuring the journey toward weight change is sustainable and reflects a genuine commitment to your personal well-being. It's not just about the number on the scale but about nurturing a lifestyle that promotes your overall well-being. It's about recognizing that the objective isn't a specific aesthetic, but rather a state of health where you feel most vibrant and capable. Because here's the crux of the matter: it's no secret that society often sees weight as a variable directly linked to perceptions of health. Height, however, is more accepted because it's assumed to be based on genetics and seen as unchangeable.

Confidence beyond the measuring tape: Have you ever found yourself wishing for an extra inch or two, or standing on tiptoes in front of the mirror? Or maybe opting for those flats instead of heels because you don't want to tower over everyone else? We just never seem to be right. But the reality is that height is a fixed attribute, with limited scope for change.

Yes, visual strategies such as posture, colors, patterns, or the use of footwear can subtly influence the perception of height. But the intrinsic value of leadership isn't measured in inches.

Nevertheless, taller leaders, on the one hand, are often seen as commanding, assertive, and more competent, yet they also struggle with assumptions that they might be intimidating or unapproachable. On the other hand, shorter leaders are seen as dynamic, agile, and approachable but often face stereotypes of lacking authority or being less capable. You just never seem to be right.

So let's see if research provides any insightful correlations between height and leadership perception.

Sylvia Ann Hewlett and her team surveyed college-educated professionals and senior executives about executive presence. They found that women are judged more critically by their weight, whereas men are more likely to be judged by their height. Of those surveyed, 16 percent said it's important for men to be tall, compared to just 6 percent for women.

According to Nancy M. Blaker and her research team, this "height premium" exists in particular across domains such as politics, business, and leadership. Daniel E. Re and his research team even found that in professional settings, taller professionals are rated as more competent leaders by others and their company's achieve higher profits.

There's actually a lot of research showing that height can be helpful in terms of perceived authority and your professional identity. However, it's crucial to remember that while being tall might influence how others perceive your leadership potential, it doesn't automatically make you a more effective real estate leader. The perception of tall leaders is based more on stereotypes than any real evidence that height enhances their leadership skills.

So, what truly defines a real estate leader? For sure, it's not solely the number on the scale or the inches on a measuring tape. It's the ability to embrace your unique physical attributes and leverage them to lead with confidence. A strong professional identity transcends physical dimensions.

Because, in the end, the real measure of your professional identity isn't found in your weight or height, but in the confidence you project. It's about being unapologetically yourself and owning your presence in every room you walk into. So stand tall, regardless of your height, and carry your weight with poise and confidence.

Leaders Are Confident about Their Age

In France, we have a special appreciation for both young and aged wines and cheeses. On the one hand, young wines and cheeses are fresh and vibrant, bringing a burst of energy and straightforward flavors to the table. They bring an immediate, joyous experience and remind us of enthusiasm and innovation. There's a sense of celebration and anticipation with young wines, as they often mark new beginnings and seasonal transitions.

On the other hand, there are aged wines and cheeses that are celebrated for their depth, complexity, and richness. They symbolize wisdom, experience, and nuanced understanding. They tell endless stories through their flavors and offer a depth of experience and a richness of character that only time can develop. Or, perhaps at this point, you might just be thinking that French people use any excuse to consume wine and cheese. And in most cases, you'd be right! But there's more to it. Because just as each wine and cheese has its unique "supposed" qualities at a certain age, so too does each stage of our professional identity.

Whether you're at the beginning of your real estate career or have decades of experience, your age is an asset that brings its own distinct value. Age, much like height and unlike weight, is an immutable number, a marker of time, but contrary to popular belief, it has no direct correlation with success. Across the spectrum of history and into the modern day, leaders have emerged at various stages of their lives, showcasing that age is not a determinant of capability. Luckily, success is age-agnostic.

Embrace the vibrancy of youth: You might be a younger real estate leader lauded for your agility, both mentally and physically. You are often seen as the vanguard of innovation, bringing fresh perspectives from recent education and a zeal for progressive methodologies. Your age represents a drive for momentum and an ambition to innovate and expand the horizons of your respective field.

Harness the wisdom of experience: Or you could be that seasoned real estate leader, whose years are viewed as a compendium of expertise, a living library of knowledge and experience garnered through years of dedication and hands-on work. Your age is often associated with a profound understanding and a reassuring presence that commands respect in any professional challenge.

Nevertheless, our age bears a psychological weight, influencing both our self-perception and the expectations of those we work with and serve.

Haven't we all, at some point in our youth, tried to look a bit older to fit in or be taken more seriously? Maybe some of us borrowed our parent's blazer or practiced our "serious face" in the mirror before that big client meeting. Others might have added a few years to their age on a dating profile or tried to sneak into a bar before they were legal. And then, as the years went by, the script flipped. Suddenly, some of us found ourselves tempted to knock a few years off our age, investing in that miracle anti-aging cream, or choosing outfits that scream "youthful and trendy" just to prove we've still got it.

It's human nature to wish to be perceived as younger or older, but challenges often arise when efforts to alter your age's perception go to extremes. Excessive attempts—such as dressing overly younger or older, extreme dieting or fitness regimens that are unsustainable, the use of heavy makeup to conceal natural features, the adoption of fashion trends that do not align with one's personal style or age, or overindulgence in plastic surgery—can convey a lack of confidence in one's natural progression through life, a message that is particularly conflicting in leadership, where authenticity and trust are paramount. These efforts, despite aiming to enhance one's appearance, may instead project a sense of insecurity, and they often backfire.

When real estate leaders resort to extreme measures to alter their age appearance, it can overshadow their actual competencies and achievements. It's a delicate balance between using visual elements to slightly improve your confidence and adjust your age's perception and overstepping into territory where those elements detract from your authenticity.

Instead, for younger real estate leaders, the focus should be on leveraging the fresh perspectives, energy, and adaptability that come with youth. It's about demonstrating a willingness to learn, innovate, and bring new ideas to the table. It involves using your unique insights and enthusiasm to drive change and inspire others, proving that age is just a number and that potential and capability are not confined by years.

Seasoned real estate leaders should establish their age-appropriate professional identity, capitalizing on the strengths that come with their experience level while challenging any perceived constraints associated with their age.

The key to navigating age is once again embracing it—owning one's years with confidence. It means celebrating milestones and viewing your age as an asset, not a barrier. Present yourself in a way that highlights the intrinsic value and unique perspective you bring to your professional role. Remember, it's not the number of years in your life or career that defines your professional identity, but rather the quality and impact of your contributions. Your age is just a number. Just a number. Period.

Leaders Are Confident about Their Gender Identity

It will come as no surprise to you that gender dynamics play a significant role in leadership perception. Hold on, pause right here, gentlemen! If you're thinking of skipping this chapter, it's time to reconsider. Navigating gender dynamics is a critical skill for every real estate leader, regardless of gender.

Traditionally, nurturing roles were seen as women's work, whereas positions of authority were for men. But today's professional world is challenging and changing those old stereotypes. Even though we've made progress, subtle shades of these stereotypes still linger, showing up in the biases and expectations that are still embedded in our workplace culture. It's an ongoing effort to root these out and move toward a truly equitable professional environment.

Women real estate leaders have shattered ceilings, but invisible barriers still hold them back. Sure, many barriers to gender equity have been broken down, often under public scrutiny that forces organizations to change. But the subtler, less visible forms of inequality still chip away at true equity. These biases are harder to spot and even harder to tackle because they're deeply woven into workplace cultures and attitudes.

So, women in leadership still have to navigate these gender-based perceptions, making sure their work's quality is the main focus, not their gender. Let's see what the research says about these gender dynamics.

Janice Fanning Madden at the University of Pennsylvania highlighted an imbalance in real estate teams within large firms. In places where income is tied to performance and commission, women, despite showing equal skills, were often given opportunities with less potential than their male counterparts. Similarly, research from Joanna Barsh and Lareina Yee at McKinsey & Company confirmed that invisible barriers are holding women back more than overt sexism.

The "Howard vs. Heidi" case study by Frank Flynn at Columbia Business School is particularly revealing. Participants were asked to evaluate profiles—identical except for the name: Howard for one group and Heidi for another. Howard was seen as competent, effective, and likable, with people eager to work with him. Heidi, despite being seen as competent and effective, wasn't met with the same warmth or enthusiasm.

This shows the bias: high-achieving women often face a stricter social ledger, where their success might actually reduce their likability—something their male counterparts don't face as often.

Charles M. Futrell's research in the *Journal of Personal Selling and Sales Management* found similar biases. Individuals assessed leadership styles on video, and their evaluations were heavily influenced by the manager's gender, regardless of the leadership approach shown. Unconscious gender biases made the same behaviors seem more or less effective depending on whether the manager was a woman or a man.

The key to overcoming these stereotypes is by embracing your gender identity with confidence and showcasing your unique leadership style. This means not feeling pressured to fit into traditionally masculine leadership modes. By cultivating a leadership identity that includes both empathy and assertiveness, you can redefine what it means to lead with influence and integrity—beyond your gender.

Gender bias has no boundaries; it affects everyone. We often talk about gender bias in terms of women, and race in terms of people of color. But what about the other groups? Defined by narrow interpretations of masculinity, men are also pressured to be decisive, tough, and unyielding, leaving little room for vulnerability or emotional openness. These standards, drilled into us from a young age through family, education, and media, can be just as restrictive and damaging.

In leadership, these pressures manifest in various ways. Male leaders might feel the need to adopt an overly aggressive leadership style, believing that showing any hesitation or uncertainty could be seen as a weakness. They might avoid asking for help or feedback, fearing it might undermine their image of competence and control. During negotiations, the pressure to be tough can lead to missed opportunities for collaboration and compromise. And the constant need to project confidence can stop male leaders from expressing doubts or discussing challenges openly, which can stifle growth and innovation.

True equality means understanding these constraints affect all genders. This includes nonbinary and transgender real estate leaders who are navigating a world that's still learning to understand and accept gender beyond the binary. Their visibility in leadership roles is itself an act of courage. For nonbinary and transgender leaders, the challenge is often about being seen and respected for their professional capabilities first, without their gender identity overshadowing their skills and contributions.

They might face inappropriate questions or comments about their gender identity, diverting attention from their professional message. Their authority might be questioned or undermined due to biases or a lack of understanding. Or they may find networking events dominated by traditional gender norms, making it hard to build relationships on an equal footing.

By focusing on professional acumen and advocating for environments where everyone is evaluated based on their abilities and contributions, we can help ensure leadership is defined by the quality of work, not by gender identity. We all play a role in pushing for policies and norms that honor gender diversity, embodying empathetic and inclusive leadership. Alongside these efforts, it's crucial to recognize how gender bias still subtly shapes our interactions and workplace culture through often unspoken microaggressions.

Embracing your gender identity as part of your leadership is a profound statement of confidence and acceptance that sets a powerful example for others. The key lies in being comfortable in your own skin and using your unique experiences to inform and enhance your leadership approach—beyond your gender. At the core of your professional reputation should always be an unwavering commitment to excellence and the quality of leadership you express.

In such an environment, gender becomes one of many aspects of a real estate leader's identity, not a hurdle to overcome but a facet that enriches your perspective.

For you, this means harmonizing your external presence with your inner identity, ensuring your professional identity reflects both your competence and your authenticity. There's no need to conform to expectations of dressing more masculine or overtly feminine. Let your gender identity enhance, not define, your leadership style.

Leaders Are Confident about Their Style

Do you have a style icon? Someone who always seems to get it right, blending consistency and creativity effortlessly? Someone who wears the same confidence every day, yet always looks fresh and different. They have that certain *je ne sais quoi*—a flair that makes heads turn and a presence that lingers long after they've left the room.

Confession time: my style icon is Iris Apfel. If you've ever seen Iris, you'll remember her for her oversized glasses, chunky jewelry, and flamboyant prints. She fascinates me. Her style is bold, unapologetic, and uniquely hers.

Yet, will you ever find me dressed up like Iris? No, because first, it's her style, not mine, and second, my environment just doesn't allow for such flamboyance. It's the everyday challenge: embracing oneself yet accepting that not all things are possible if you interact in a professional environment that demands a different approach.

Yet even in a professional environment, there's plenty of room to weave in distinctive elements that set your style apart. The key is balance: your style should never overshadow your competencies but rather complement and enhance your professional narrative. This means understanding what style is not, as much as what it is.

- **Style isn't about mimicking others;** it's about discovering your own unique expression. It's not about seeking validation from others; it's about feeling empowered and comfortable in your own choices.

- **Style isn't just about color or fit;** it's about the message you want to send, rooted in the values you want to project—confidence, approachability, innovation, tradition, creativity, care—and how these are encapsulated in your visual presence. It's a broader expression of your identity and offers a glimpse into your personality without uttering a single word.

- **Style isn't about chasing the whims of fashion** or flaunting the price tags of luxury brands. It's not about squeezing into the latest silhouette or echoing the masses. It's about embracing timeless elegance and quality that reflect your personal values and essence.

- **Style doesn't demand perfection;** it's not a one-size-fits-all formula. It's not about dressing to impress others or putting on a costume for approval. True style transcends trends and societal expectations; it's an individual expression that remains steady over time, unaffected by public opinion.

In the real estate world, your style acts as a visual signature, making you easily recognizable and memorable. Here mastering your style means understanding that going overboard can be counterproductive.

It's not about pushing boundaries to the extreme but pushing them just enough to be intriguing and, above all, true to yourself. Because your style shouldn't distract; it should fascinate. It shouldn't raise questions; it should assert confidence.

It could be the elegance of a custom-tailored blazer, the strategic selection of an accessory, or the timeless charm of a statement piece of jewelry. It's in the carefully chosen tie clip commemorating a personal triumph, the glimpse of an unexpected pattern on a shirt, or the pop of color from a pocket square that enlivens a traditional outfit. It's the distinctive design of your watch or the choice of vibrant socks signaling a meticulous eye for detail. These elements shouldn't scream for attention but invite intrigue and respect.

Defining your personal style can be challenging. Unlike pursuing a specific niche in your real estate career, which may be influenced by passion, skill, or opportunity, style is more abstract and deeply personal. It's an introspective process to determine how you want to present yourself and be perceived by the world.

The question "What's your style?" can often leave real estate leaders pondering. Style is complex and requires many questions to be answered before you can confidently define it, such as the following:

- Does your style amplify your voice?
- How does your style make you feel about yourself?
- How does it affect your confidence?
- Are there unique elements that make your style memorable?
- Does your style incorporate elements of your personality?
- Can your style evolve while maintaining your core identity?
- Does it reflect your leadership capabilities?
- How does your style influence your team's perception of you?
- Is your style practical and functional for your daily activities?
- How does your style align with your brokerage's branding and culture?

- How does your style adapt to different real estate contexts?
- How does your style bridge or speak to diverse client backgrounds?
- How do your style choices reflect your commitment to quality and attention to detail?

Only by answering these questions can you begin to craft a style narrative that is unique and aligns with your best self, leading to a style and professional identity that consistently and coherently communicates who you are at your core. It's about selecting pieces that enhance your visual presence and resonate with who you are, your values, and the message you wish to convey. This journey might be challenging, but the result is a style that genuinely reflects your inner self and professional ethos.

There is no shortcut to developing a true sense of style. The key is finding ways to express your real estate zeal and personalized flair through intentional choices that enhance, not distract. It's about cultivating a coherent, intentional style alignment between an individual and a brokerage image without compromising taste or propriety.

By avoiding heavy-handed themes, a real estate leader demonstrates a nuanced understanding of embodying a brand's identity with polish and self-assuredness, letting genuine passion and expertise shine through in elegant yet impactful ways.

So, take the time to explore and refine your personal style. Wear it with confidence and pride. Let it reflect the real estate leader you are and the impact you aim to make in your industry and beyond. Your style is uniquely yours. Own it, refine it, and let it shine as a reflection of the exceptional real estate leader you are.

Chapter 4
Leaders Look Authentic

The Art of Standing Out
While Fitting In,
Without Disappearing.

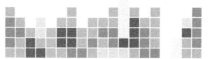

Chapter 4:
Leaders Look Authentic

Let's venture into the fascinating world of animals once again and take a look at two other remarkable creatures. First, picture a chameleon. This little reptile, with its googly eyes and color-changing skin, is nature's ultimate shape-shifter. It can blend seamlessly into any environment—lush green leaves or sandy desert tones. It's not just hiding; it's communicating, regulating temperature, and surviving. The chameleon is a master of adaptation. But here's the catch: in all that blending, its true self is often hidden beneath those shifting colors, rarely showing its genuine hues. Now, imagine a peacock. With its dazzling feathers and extravagant display, the peacock is all about showing off. It struts around, flaunting its stunning array of colors for everyone to see. The peacock doesn't blend in; it stands out—boldly and unapologetically. Its showy display screams health, vitality, and confidence. But while the peacock's feathers attract admiration, they also make it an easy target for predators.

In the real estate world, leaders face a similar dilemma. Should they be like the chameleon, blending in and adapting to every situation, or like the peacock, boldly displaying their true selves?

Being a chameleon in real estate means constantly adjusting your professional identity to fit into different contexts and expectations. This adaptability can be a great asset, especially in diverse and dynamic environments.

But there's a downside: you might lose sight of your true self. When you're always changing to match your surroundings, you risk that your unique contributions become overshadowed by your desire to fit in.

On the flip side, being a peacock means showcasing your true self with confidence and flair. This approach can make you memorable and earn you respect for your individuality and courage. But there's a catch here too. In a real estate setting that values conformity and predictability, being too much of a peacock can make you seem out of touch. It's easy to be seen as more concerned with making a statement than with achieving the team's goals.

So, how do you strike the right balance?

The pursuit of authenticity has become a rallying cry for real estate leaders across all sectors. But what does it really mean to be an authentic real estate leader in today's high-stakes environment? Is it about unfiltered self-expression, or is there a more nuanced approach that balances personal identity with professional expectations?

Authenticity is a term that gets tossed around a lot. At its core, being authentic means being true to your own personality, spirit, or character. Yet it's a concept that's far more nuanced than simply "being yourself." Ignoring your environment and the context in which you operate can lead to a dangerous misconception about authenticity, one that is especially prevalent in the advice of "You do you!" This notion suggests being authentic means you can do, say, or wear whatever you want, regardless of the situation. It's advice that, admittedly, many of us have given and received as well, including myself.

However, this belief fails to recognize the importance of aligning your authentic self with the expectations and norms of your professional setting. When you disregard the context and operate solely on the principle of "You do you," you risk coming across as tone-deaf or even disrespectful, which can be a costly mistake.

It can give off the impression that you don't care about anyone or anything, anywhere, at any time.

Let me share some uncomfortable truths with you.

Authenticity is not an excuse for disregarding norms. The reality is that authenticity does not exist in a vacuum. Just as the chameleon adapts to its environment while maintaining its core essence, real estate leaders operate within a complex network of relationships, expectations, and social norms. While it's important to stay true to your core, you must also recognize your self-expression has an impact on those around you.

Using authenticity as a justification for ignoring any and all professional norms risks damaging the very relationships and trust that are essential to success as a real estate leader. When you disregard these norms in the name of authenticity, you can come across as unprofessional, untrustworthy, or even arrogant.

This doesn't mean you need to completely suppress your individuality. Rather, it's about finding a way to express your authentic self within the framework of your professional context.

There is no such thing as one singular authentic self. The second notion that we each have one "authentic self"—sorry to break the news—is a lie. Just like the chameleon, we need to adapt to numerous roles in life. We're parents, siblings, children, friends, neighbors, colleagues—and real estate leaders. Each of these roles demands a different facet of our presentation. Imagine interacting with your children in the same way as with your clients, or speaking to your parents as you would to your life partner. Wearing the same outfit in the gym as you would at a property showing. Although there may be a consistent thread of core values and beliefs that define you, the expression of your authenticity will naturally vary depending on the situation.

Authenticity, then, is not about a rigid adherence to a single, unchanging self in all contexts. The focus is on being true to your core values while also possessing the flexibility to effectively navigate different environments.

In leadership, this means finding harmony between your private persona and your professional identity, ensuring each role you play is infused with your values. It's not about concealing who you are; it's about respectfully acknowledging the part you play in each aspect and role of your life and doing so with sincerity and professionalism.

Authenticity is not a fixed state. Many leaders believe that once they discover their authentic self, they're set for life. They think that authenticity is a destination, a place they arrive at and never have to leave. But the truth is, authenticity is a journey, not a final stop.

As we navigate through our careers and life, we are constantly growing, learning, and evolving. Our experiences shape us, our relationships change us, and our perspectives shift. As a result, our understanding of ourselves and how we express our authenticity also evolves. What felt authentic to us in our twenties may not feel the same way in our forties or sixties.

Peacocks do not develop their striking tail feathers right away. When they are born, peachicks are covered in a dull, brown plumage that provides camouflage and protection from predators. It takes years until they develop their characteristic tail feathers, and their colors continue to change as they mature.

You need to regularly reassess and adjust your authentic expression. You need to take the time to check in with yourself, to ask if the way you're presenting yourself to the world still aligns with your core values. It's a process of continuous self-discovery and self-alignment. One that means recognizing what made us authentic real estate leaders in the past may not be what makes us authentic leaders in the present or future.

Authenticity is not an excuse for being unfiltered. There's a common misconception that to be authentic, you must share every detail of your life and thoughts, holding nothing back. But this couldn't be further from the truth.

Think about the peacock again. Its bold display is carefully chosen and not everything is on show at all times. Authenticity is about being true to yourself, but it doesn't mean you have to reveal every aspect of your life to everyone. Instead, authenticity is about being transparent about the things that matter, while also maintaining appropriate boundaries.

These boundaries are often crafted by the implicit expectations and unspoken scripts that permeate every industry and society at large. Like invisible guardrails, they guide and shape perceptions, influencing how others view and interpret your actions, words, and appearance. Society has preconceived notions of what a real estate leader should look like, sound like, and act like. These scripts, while rarely explicitly stated, carry significant weight in how your authenticity is perceived and received. And your visual appearance can either confirm or challenge these scripts.

During my keynotes, I present participants with various images of individuals dressed in professional attire. I then pose a question to the audience: Which of these individuals would you entrust with your legal battles, your computer setup, or the education of your children? Again and again, the responses are predictably consistent, underscoring how quickly we form perceptions based on someone's visual appearance only. My audiences' inner dialogue might go something like this: The sharp lines of that charcoal-gray suit, the impeccable white shirt, and the red tie exude a strategic and commanding presence—that's got to be the lawyer. Right next to that person is someone in smart casual attire—a coat, a light shirt without a tie, and slacks. Clearly, that's the IT expert. Then there's someone in a light, pastel dress that flows softly, the kind that suggests kindness and a nurturing spirit; surely, she's the teacher.

Every time my audience seems surprised that they share the same opinions. Witchcraft, once again, they might think. But the reality is much simpler: I'm just tapping into and leveraging the preexisting scripts in their minds.

It's not magic; it's the power of subconscious visual cues and deeply ingrained stereotypes. Let's dive into these mental scripts and see which ones you might be adhering to or have internalized. Understanding these patterns can empower you to strategically align your professional identity with your authentic self.

Keywords Are the Keys to Authenticity

Every industry has a mental "uniform"—a sartorial standard that might not be as overt and codified as those for police officers, firefighters, or chefs, but it's implicitly understood. These are the "perceived uniforms," an unspoken dress code shaped by societal expectations and assumptions about certain professions. These perceived uniforms serve as a visual shorthand, helping to forge an immediate connection between professional identity and public perception. While they are complex in their detail, I simplify them by applying keywords to these mental uniforms.

You might ask: So, what are the expected keywords in my real estate field and for my mental uniform? The answer lies in the collective expectations of all stakeholders—clients, team members, colleagues, upper management, media, the general public—who interact with you. These keywords become the essence of the perceived uniform for you.

By carefully crafting a professional identity that aligns with these keywords, you can craft a perception that not only meets professional standards but also resonates with the unique characteristics of your field—thereby reinforcing your role and strengthening your personal identity.

Cracking your field's keywords and your profession's DNA: The first step in crafting your personal and professional style is to identify the keywords associated with your real estate field or profession. These keywords encapsulate the core values, traits, and expectations that define success in your field.

To determine your real estate field's or profession's keywords, consider the following questions:

- What are the primary goals and objectives in your field?
- What are the core values that underpin your field?
- What are the most significant trends shaping your field?
- What are the unique selling propositions in your field?
- What expectations do clients and stakeholders have of leaders in your field?
- What words or phrases are commonly used to describe your field in media, marketing, or public discourse?
- What qualities do the most influential figures in your field embody?

By reflecting on these questions and observing the standards within your real estate field, you can begin to identify the keywords that define your field's or profession's perceived uniform.

Defining your distinctive edge and personal keywords: The most authentic real estate leaders understand they can convey a narrative about who they are with their visual presence, and they're clear about the keywords that describe this narrative. Each keyword tells a part of their story. Each look confirms the essence of their story.

If your professional ethos is grounded in dependability, expertise, and commitment, your professional identity should reinforce these qualities visually. Alternatively, if you pride yourself on being pioneering, bold, and inventive, your visual choices might be more daring and innovative, reflecting a trailblazing spirit.

Have you considered the unique traits that define you in your real estate role and how they translate into the visual messages you wish to instantly imprint? It's the most crucial step. Because doing so allows you to pinpoint a style that not only makes you feel confident but also conveys the key messages you intend to communicate with your professional identity.

Harmonizing your field's expectations and your personal essence: Once your real estate field's (or industry's, brokerage's, profession's, or specific role's) keywords and your personal keywords are established, the next phase is alignment—that is, checking whether these keywords echo and resonate with each other. If you are fortunate, the keywords you have selected to describe your authentic self align with the persona expected in your professional sphere. When there's a match, it can feel like a natural extension of your identity.

Conversely, if there's a disconnect, it can manifest as a nagging sense of being out of place, prompting you to question why you feel like you don't quite belong. These are the real estate leaders who often find themselves at a crossroads, grappling with the tension between their authentic selves and the expectations of their roles. They may feel like they're constantly putting on a mask, suppressing parts of themselves to fit into a mold that doesn't quite fit. This internal dissonance can lead to feelings of frustration, burnout, and even a loss of purpose.

On the flip side, when there's alignment between both keywords, these are the real estate leaders who tend to thrive. They exude a sense of ease and confidence in their roles, as if they were born to do what they do. Their authenticity shines through effortlessly, and they have a way of inspiring and motivating others simply by being themselves.

This alignment allows them to bring their whole selves to their work, tapping into a deep well of intrinsic motivation and passion. They don't feel the need to compartmentalize or hide parts of themselves, because their authentic identity is not just accepted but celebrated in their professional context.

Emerging from the myriad of possible keywords and attributes are seven distinct perception personas. Each of these personas is like a unique flavor, representing a specific set of values and traits that real estate leaders either naturally embody or are expected to adopt in their roles.

But here's the thing—these personas go way beyond just clothing choices. They represent the holistic professional identity that real estate leaders are anticipated to uphold in their work and interactions.

Now, let's break them down. The seven personas can be categorized into two types: your primary and your secondary persona.

- **Your primary persona is like your professional backbone**—akin to your DNA and the core of your identity. It's reflected in the consistent threads of your character, influencing your instinctive choices and the way you inherently engage with the world.

- **Your secondary persona is more fluid and adaptable**—sculpted by the ebb and flow of your external experiences, age, education, preferences, and the continuous curve of personal and professional development. It grants you the flexibility to adapt, to mold your choices to fit the myriad of scenarios you encounter throughout your real estate career and life.

While your primary persona remains steadfast, your secondary persona acts as a versatile sidekick. It doesn't overshadow your core; instead, it enhances it, allowing you a wider range of expression. Together, they form a cohesive identity that is both true to your essence and attuned to your professional environment.

Before we jump into outlining the personas, it's crucial to understand that these personas are not rigid boxes. They're more than just labels. They influence our perspective on the world, and, consequently, these personas often manifest in our external presentation—the clothes we choose, the hairstyles we adopt, and the accessories we carry. All of these are outward expressions of our inner narrative. And you might find yourself resonating with more than just one primary or secondary persona—but we'll get to that complexity later.

It's also important to recognize that while I use elements of each persona's visual appearance to describe them, their traits permeate into behavior, communication, digital presence, and environment. These personas are holistic, encompassing not just how one looks, but how one acts, interacts, and presents themselves in all aspects of their professional lives.

However, it's often through our visual appearance that we get the first strong indication of how these personas express their unique keywords. One's looks serve as the initial canvas upon which they paint the picture of who they are and what they stand for. Their visual appearance is like the opening scene in the movie of their professional identity, setting the tone and creating expectations for the interactions to come. But just like in a movie, their story goes beyond the opening scene. Their visual presence is just the beginning. It's through their actions, words, and the way they engage with the world around them that the full depth and complexity of their persona is revealed.

So, are you ready to explore the three primary personas that exist?

The Explorer: Approachable and Relaxed

Explorers embody a spirit that is both adventurous and pragmatic, often reflected in a style that prioritizes comfort and practicality. They choose their wardrobe less for the latest fashion trends and more for the functionality and durability of the garments. Imagine their attire as ready for an impromptu client visit because it is for a casual business meeting: comfortable slacks paired with a resilient button-down shirt and sturdy footwear that speaks to a life in motion.

In their wardrobe, you'll find clothes, many in earthy tones, that serve a purpose: utility jackets with pockets aplenty, fabrics that can withstand the elements, and colors that blend with the natural world.

Maintenance is fuss-free, with a preference for clothing that endures the wear and tear of their leadership adventures without demanding meticulous care.

Their approach to body image is straightforward and unpretentious. Their physique, whether it's conditioned by active pursuits or carries the robustness of a life well lived, is a testament to their experiences rather than a curated image. In their world, the body is less a canvas for fashion and more a vessel for adventure, a mindset that brings a unique confidence and an unbothered attitude toward societal beauty standards.

When it comes to grooming, the Explorer favors a minimalistic approach, if any at all. A touch of moisturizer for a healthy glow, a swipe of clear lip balm, and a simple hairstyle are all they need to maintain their natural look, ready for whatever the leadership day may bring.

Their accessories, like the sporty watch on their wrist to the durable briefcase slung over their shoulder, are chosen for resilience and utility, echoing the Explorer's readiness for life's spontaneous leadership adventures.

For hair and nails, the Explorer opts for easy maintenance, prioritizing health and manageability. A simple, practical haircut suits their active lifestyle. Their manicure and pedicure are neat yet unfussy, often favoring clear polish or natural tones that don't show wear easily.

- **Keyword:** comfort
- **Perceived traits:** active, adventurous, casual, approachable, optimistic, energetic, natural, direct, spontaneous, enthusiastic
- **Perceived challenges:** disorganized, dull, graceless, mannerless, ordinary, unambitious, unpolished, weak

This persona shines in real estate roles that need an approachable, down-to-earth presence and the ability to effortlessly move between formal and casual settings.

Imagine industries such as residential real estate, property management, or real estate photography/videography. The Explorer's adventurous spirit and practical approach make them a great fit. Their easy-going nature helps them connect with clients and team members alike, fostering a sense of camaraderie.

Or, in the world of real estate startups, entrepreneurial ventures, or real estate technology, the Explorer's casual confidence is a huge asset. They come across as accessible and relatable, someone who's in the trenches with their team. This lack of pretense helps build strong relationships and shows they're ready to roll up their sleeves and get to work.

Or, for real estate roles in industrial, land acquisition, or urban planning sectors, the Explorer's practicality is a perfect match too. Their hands-on approach and no-nonsense attitude resonate well in these fields. They embody the durability and resilience that these sectors value.

However, the Explorer might find it challenging to thrive in highly formal and image-conscious roles such as high-end luxury residential, commercial real estate investment, or real estate law. These fields often require a more polished and refined professional identity, which can be at odds with the Explorer's preference for comfort and practicality. In these environments, the Explorer's style might easily be perceived as too casual or unrefined.

The Traditionalist: Trustworthy and Reliable

The Traditionalist carries an air of timeless elegance, exuding a commitment to enduring styles that is immediately apparent. They aren't swayed by passing trends but are firmly rooted in classic fashion principles.

Envision them in attire that pays homage to the past while fitting impeccably into the now: a well-tailored suit that defies the ebb and flow of fads, a crisp dress shirt that whispers decades of sophistication, and leather shoes polished to perfection.

In their wardrobe, you will discover a carefully selected ensemble of pieces that defy the transient whims of fashion, privileging enduring quality and craftsmanship. Each item is tended to meticulously, ensuring their presentation is as flawless as it is in honor of their conservative sensibilities.

Their perspective on body image is in harmony with this classic sense of style. The Traditionalist presents themselves in a manner that conveys diligent self-care and a refined composure, regardless of their body type. Their physique reflects a devotion to a persona that upholds their values—subtle yet unmistakably dignified.

When it comes to grooming, the Traditionalist opts for the timeless. A neat hairstyle, a clean shave or well-trimmed facial hair, and a subtle fragrance that serve more as a tribute to poise than a pursuit of the spotlight.

Their accessories are chosen with discretion, from the understated elegance of their cuff links to the classic lines of their wristwatch. As for hair and nail care, they select styles that stand the test of time—perhaps a sleek side part or a classic manicure. Their nails are impeccably groomed, often in clear or neutral polish, complementing their wardrobe's timeless grace.

- **Keyword:** values
- **Perceived traits:** trustworthy, loyal, organized, practical, consistent, dependable, responsible, reliable, conscientious, appropriate
- **Perceived challenges:** authoritarian, boring, conformist, inflexible, elitist, predictable, reserved, uncreative

The Traditionalist persona finds its ideal expression in leadership roles that prioritize deep client trust and unshakable credibility. The Traditionalist's commitment to timeless principles tends to be an asset in more conservative, legacy-minded real estate sectors.

For instance, in commercial real estate investment, real estate law, or real estate accounting, the Traditionalist's classic approach helps foster perceptions of fiscal responsibility and legal acumen, which are crucial for earning stakeholder buy-in.

Similarly, in executive roles within long-established real estate firms, real estate associations, or real estate education, the Traditionalist persona aligns well with conducting business with utmost formality and adherence to decorum.

Leadership roles that require the ability to impress authorities or clients who deeply value custom, propriety, and hard-earned reputations over flashiness are ideal for the Traditionalist too, such as high-end residential real estate, luxury property management, or historic property restoration.

However, Traditionalists might find it challenging to thrive in more dynamic, fast-paced real estate sectors that value innovation and a cutting-edge approach. Their adherence to classic and conservative principles might be perceived as outdated or too rigid in these environments, such as in proptech startups, creative real estate marketing, or avant-garde architectural design.

The Cosmopolitan: Sophisticated and Eloquent

The Cosmopolitan is an embodiment of luxury and refinement, a sartorial symphony in which each element harmonizes with their sophisticated lifestyle.

Their wardrobe is a subtle murmur of opulence. Designer brands and lavish pieces are selected not merely for their aesthetic allure but also for their ability to broadcast an air of exclusivity and global sophistication. Their wardrobe maintenance mirrors their dedication to a life well-curated, with each garment receiving the meticulous care needed to maintain its premium appearance.

Their view on body image is anchored in elegance. The Cosmopolitan considers their physique as a canvas for high fashion, with each silhouette gracefully adorned in fine materials.

The manner in which they carry themself—a synthesis of poise and self-assurance—enhances their impeccable taste in clothing.

When it comes to grooming, they strike the perfect balance between understated and impactful, crafting a visage that speaks of refinement and luxury. A perfect hairstyle, a hint of color in their accessories, subtle fragrance, and a well-manicured appearance that adds just the right touch of sophistication.

Accessories for them are more than adornments; they are declarations of quality and craftsmanship that articulate their discerning preferences.

Their grooming, including hair and nails, follows the philosophy of "less is more"—as long as it's exquisite. Elegant hairstyles that frame their face and a manicure that boasts of subtle, neutral tones or a classic style. These choices are intentional, serving not just as aspects of their personal upkeep but as integral parts of their social signature.

Every facet of their appearance, from meticulous skin care routines to the selection of a signature scent, is a conscious act in shaping a professional identity that vibrates with the core of high society.

- **Keyword:** quality
- **Perceived traits:** distinguished, proper, notable, cultivated, refined, meticulous, discerning, dignified, excellent
- **Perceived challenges:** arrogant, bossy, calculating, decadent, impersonal, intolerant, stiff, uncaring

The Cosmopolitan persona thrives in leadership roles that demand a touch of refinement and global sophistication. Think about luxury residential real estate, high-end commercial real estate investment, or exclusive property management—whether it's private estates, top-tier office spaces, luxury resorts, or other upscale properties. The Cosmopolitan's polished and cultured style aligns seamlessly with the aspirational ethos of these sectors.

In fields such as high-end architectural design or exclusive real estate investment trusts, the Cosmopolitan's worldly elegance and impeccable poise exude the jet-setting sensibilities and white-glove service standards these elite clients expect.

For those in leadership catering to ultra-high-net-worth individuals, the Cosmopolitan's elevated tastes and attention to detail resonate perfectly with discerning clients looking for the most prestigious properties and bespoke experiences.

This persona also shines in real estate roles related to luxury lifestyle branding, such as in marketing for high-end residential developments, exclusive golf communities, or private island resorts. Their elegant self-presentation mirrors the artisanal craftsmanship and uncompromising quality that define these marquee properties.

In any leadership context where the hallmarks of luxury, prestige, and exclusivity drive client decisions and shape the market, the Cosmopolitan commands attention and credibility.

However, Cosmopolitans might face challenges in more casual or utilitarian real estate sectors. Fields that value practicality and a hands-on approach, such as industrial real estate, land development, or affordable housing initiatives, often require a more rugged and straightforward presentation. In such settings, the Cosmopolitan's focus on luxury and refinement may come across as overly extravagant or disconnected from the practical realities of these sectors.

Now remember, there is no right or wrong type of primary persona. Each persona, be it the Explorer, Traditionalist, or Cosmopolitan, comes with its unique set of strengths and challenges. Whether you resonate with the unbound spirit of the Explorer, the steadfast resolve of the Traditionalist, or the sophisticated flair of the Cosmopolitan, each brings its distinctive palette of perceived traits and challenges. Yet, remember, your primary persona is the quintessence of your being, the inherent nature you carry from the cradle to the crescendo of your real estate career.

It's the unchanging core that defines your authentic self, and it's not something you should attempt to alter.

A Cosmopolitan attempting to mimic the Explorer's casual conduct, or an Explorer trying to copy the Traditionalist's formality, will often feel uncomfortable, just like an ill-fitting garment. This incongruence can radiate subtle cues of inauthenticity, leaving you and others with a sense of dissonance and sensing that something is amiss, even if they can't pinpoint exactly what it is.

Instead, your adaptability comes from your secondary personas—the versatile facets of your identity that you've honed through experience, environment, and personal and professional development. These are the aspects you can shift and shape more. They enable you to purposefully imprint traits and characteristics onto others, facilitating instant connections without sacrificing the integrity of your true self. However, the four secondary personas are not about changing who you are but about expanding the ways you can authentically showcase yourself to the world.

The Caregiver: Supportive and Nurturing

The Caregiver's style resonates with a delicate finesse. These are the real estate leaders who thread warmth and nurturing into every interaction. In their wardrobe, you'll find fine, small patterns and soft fabrics that offer comfort both to themselves and those they encounter. Soft colors such as pastels are prevalent, reflecting their gentle nature and contributing to a calming atmosphere wherever they go.

Caregivers curate a wardrobe that melds professional expectations with a personal touch. Shirts with delicate details, cardigans in soothing hues, and tailored slacks or skirts exemplify their effortless grace. Their clothing is not merely a uniform but a testament to their role as a nurturer, blending the demands of their profession with innate compassion.

In their body image, the Caregiver appreciates subtlety and health, finding beauty in the natural and the genuine. Their physical presence is characterized by an understated grace, maintaining a physique that speaks to vitality and genuine care rather than vanity.

For the Caregiver, accessories and personal grooming are reflective of their tender approach to life. Jewelry is minimal and meaningful, shoes are chosen for comfort yet display quiet elegance or small embellishments, and grooming is consistent with their overall ethos: thoughtful and impeccably maintained.

When it comes to grooming, they approach it as they do their role—enhancing features softly and naturally, ensuring their presence is as reassuring as the support they offer. Their hair is often styled in a way that's practical yet inviting, perhaps a soft style or gentle waves, and their nails are kept clean and neatly groomed, often in muted or clear tones.

- **Keyword:** care
- **Perceived traits:** supportive, caring, warm, nurturing, considerate, compassionate, gentle, soft-spoken, receptive, demure
- **Perceived challenges:** anxious, emotional, dependent, insecure, noncompetitive, naïve, passive, undemanding, hesitant

The Caregiver persona finds its strongest calling in leadership roles within sectors that place a premium on empathetic client guidance, emotional sensitivity, and cultivating an authentic spirit of care and compassion.

Hence, this persona is a natural fit in residential real estate, especially in roles involving first-time homebuyers, family relocations, or senior living transitions. Here, the Caregiver's nurturing nature brings intrinsic credibility, creating trust and comfort during these emotionally charged real estate journeys.

For real estate roles in community development, affordable housing initiatives, or nonprofit housing associations, the Caregiver embodies the heartfelt investment and delicate handling required by these socially conscious endeavors.

In property management roles, particularly in residential communities, assisted living facilities, or student housing, the Caregiver's genuine concern for residents' well-being and their ability to handle sensitive situations with care are invaluable assets.

The Caregiver persona also shines in real estate education and training, from mentoring new agents to leading professional development programs, where their supportive and empathetic nature fosters growth and learning.

In any leadership context where emotional intelligence, empathy, and a care-centric approach are essential, the Caregiver provides incomparable guidance.

However, Caregivers might find it challenging to thrive in highly competitive and more aggressive real estate environments that prioritize hard-nosed negotiation and the relentless pursuit of profits. Sectors such as commercial real estate investment, land speculation, or high-stakes property development often require a more assertive and results-driven approach. In these settings, the Caregiver's emphasis on empathy and nurturing may be perceived as a lack of competitiveness or decisiveness.

The Avant-Garde: Individualistic and Creative

The Avant-Garde stands as a testament to their creativity and self-expression, valuable in real estate sectors that prize innovation, such as in cutting-edge architectural design, innovative urban planning, or forward-thinking real estate technology. Their appearance is a vibrant tapestry of artistic exploration, with a wardrobe that narrates stories of bold experimentation and the redefining of boundaries.

They select audacious colors, embrace emerging designers, and favor unique silhouettes that are the hallmarks of their style—a visual celebration of their commitment to pushing the frontiers of fashion. The maintenance of their wardrobe is an act of artistic devotion, each piece cared for with precision or sometimes creatively repurposed in their ongoing narrative.

The Avant-Garde views their physique as a medium for artistic display, embracing a spectrum of styles that challenge conventional beauty norms. They wear their confidence as effortlessly as their eclectic mix of garments, radiating a presence that commands attention and sparks dialogue. They approach their health with an artistic flair, aligning their physical activities and mental wellness practices with their creative life, even if it means deviating from conventional health routines.

Their accessories, from their statement jewelry to their sculptural shoes, are not mere embellishments but proclamations of their originality, each chosen for its unique design and the conversation it incites.

Their grooming routines are an extension of their creative ethos. Grooming is an opportunity for innovation, and hair and nail care become expressions of their Avant-garde identity, transcending the typical to become part of their artistic statement. Every element of their appearance is a deliberate choice, a chapter in the creative odyssey they embody, inviting all to witness the living art they present to the world.

- **Keyword:** creativity
- **Perceived traits:** innovative, imaginative, free-spirited, independent, original, unique, unconventional, fearless, impromptu
- **Perceived challenges:** unrealistic, undisciplined, opinionated, neglectful, inconsistent, disruptive, contrary, awkward

The Avant-Garde's unconventional creativity thrives in real estate arenas that celebrate bold visionaries and innovative artistic leaders. Think of groundbreaking architectural firms, cutting-edge urban design, or inventive proptech as their playgrounds. The Avant-Garde essence captivates early adopters hungry for visionary ideas that push the boundaries of what's possible in real estate.

In real estate marketing and branding agencies, the Avant-Garde persona embodies the pioneering philosophies and boundary-defying ethos these sectors cherish. Their artistic self-expression and nonconformist attitude align perfectly with the demand for disruptive creative solutions in property marketing and brand identity.

Real estate development roles that involve conceptualizing and designing innovative living spaces, such as eco-friendly communities, mixed-use developments, or smart cities, allow the Avant-Garde to channel their creative energy into shaping the future of how we live, work, and play.

Similarly, in real estate sectors that intersect with art and culture, such as developing art districts, cultural centers, or creative live–work spaces, the Avant-Garde is uniquely equipped to convey a deep appreciation for groundbreaking creative movements and translate that into the built environment.

In any leadership context that celebrates limitless creativity, inspired innovation, and design-forward futurism, the Avant-Garde persona shines at their genre-defying best.

However, Avant-Gardes might find it challenging to thrive in highly regulated or traditional real estate sectors that prioritize conformity and adherence to established norms. Fields such as real estate law, real estate accounting, or conventional residential property management often expect a more conventional and disciplined approach. The Avant-Garde's emphasis on creativity and nonconformity may be perceived as disruptive or unprofessional in these more traditional environments.

The Glamorous: Magnetic and Extravagant

The Glamorous persona is a paragon of attention and fashion, making them a natural fit for roles in luxury real estate marketing, high-end property staging, or celebrity real estate representation. Their wardrobe is a bastion of opulence, each piece resonating with the allure of a meticulously curated collection.

Picture them in attire that captivates with its shimmering details, reflective finishes, and a bold color palette—from the fierceness of reds to the solemnity of blacks and the nobility of purples. When it comes to maintaining their wardrobe, they exercise some care, trying to preserve each piece as a cherished element of their sumptuous attire. If it doesn't, no worries, they'll just move on to the next fashion item.

They regard their body as integral to their personal identity; they sculpt their physique to harmonize with their taste and social stature. Their fitness routines are as much a part of their brand narrative as their choice of wardrobe, enhancing their aesthetic and their presence.

Their accessories are selected for their storytelling power and their ability to accentuate their captivating presence. These pieces, however, don't have to be luxurious jewelry or high-end designer shoes. What matters more than the price tag is how much attention the piece can possibly draw to their look.

Their grooming routines are conducted with the same precision and intentionality as dressing for a gala. Grooming for them is artistry, hair care is a discipline, and skin care is a devotion, each facet executed to radiate charisma and draw admiration. This scrupulous cultivation of their appearance reflects a profound appreciation for the transformative power of appearance.

- **Keyword:** attraction
- **Perceived traits:** trendy, stimulating, popular, magnetic, fit, extravagant, daring, attractive, admirable

- **Perceived challenges:** pompous, one-dimensional, manipulative, insincere, indiscreet, flamboyant, deceitful, artificial

The Glamorous persona truly thrives in real estate–related roles that revolve around high visibility and image-driven sectors. Their magnetic persona aligns seamlessly with professions where visual appeal, public presence, and stylish presentation are paramount.

In real estate media and entertainment, the Glamorous persona is perfect for hosting real estate television shows, producing engaging social media content, and acting as a charismatic spokesperson for high-profile properties. Their flair for presentation and captivating storytelling makes them ideal for showcasing properties and lifestyle experiences.

In interior design, the Glamorous persona excels in roles such as luxury home stagers or interior decorators for high-end properties. Their eye for aesthetics and dedication to creating picture-perfect spaces enhance the visual appeal and marketability of exclusive properties.

As brand ambassadors for real estate companies or high-end developments, the Glamorous persona's magnetism makes them ideal representatives. They effortlessly draw attention, making them perfect for marketing campaigns, promotional events, and public relations efforts.

In the realm of social media, the Glamorous persona can shine as influencers or content creators, using their platforms to promote exclusive properties, share design inspirations, and engage with a broad audience. Their ability to create visually appealing and aspirational content helps in building a strong online presence for real estate brands.

Real estate branding and marketing, focused on crafting aspirational lifestyle narratives for high-end developments, also benefit from the Glamorous essence.

They convey the irresistible allure and prestige that affluent buyers desire, making any property or development more captivating.

However, the Glamorous might find it challenging to thrive in real estate sectors that prioritize practicality, affordability, or a more grounded, relatable approach. These fields, such as budget-friendly residential properties, low-income housing initiatives, or no-frills commercial spaces, require a more straightforward and utilitarian approach. Additionally, very traditional real estate sectors, where conservative practices and understated professionalism are valued, may also find the emphasis on extravagance and glamour to be excessive or out of touch with the needs and expectations of these markets.

The Dramatic: Strong and Fearless

The Dramatic persona is an unforgettable presence, embodying a love for the bold and theatrical that can be harnessed in roles from high-stakes commercial real estate negotiations to luxury property auctions. Their wardrobe is an audacious array of statement pieces that seize attention, mirroring the boldness of their personality.

Their wardrobe is a testament to their fearlessness, with each item chosen for its impact. It's fashion that doesn't just capture the limelight—it generates it, ensuring they aren't just observed but remembered. Architectural collars, oversized sleeves, and other unconventional silhouettes are their staples, each piece a statement in itself. They revel in the strength and sophistication of black, black, and then some more black, allowing it to dominate their wardrobe as the color of their joy. When they opt for other colors, it's strategically employed to forge a stark, memorable contrast that complements their daring sartorial narrative.

The maintenance of their wardrobe is as exacting and dramatic as a theater's costume shop: detailed, intentional, and always in pursuit of the remarkable.

They view their body as a stage for a commanding performance. Their confidence is their most treasured garment, enveloping a physique that is as dynamic as their sartorial choices, making a statement as memorable as their own dramatic essence.

Their accessories and grooming routines are essential to their expressive arsenal. Each piece of jewelry, every selection of shoes, and every grooming choice is a thoughtful act of self-expression, adding bold lines to the story they embody.

For the Dramatic, the world is a vast stage, and they are always in the lead role, with each facet of their appearance carefully curated to etch a lasting impression of their indelible presence in any professional setting.

- **Keyword:** power
- **Perceived traits:** strong, intense, charismatic, demanding, bold, commanding, captivating, aloof, severe, spectacular
- **Perceived challenges:** tough, possessive, intrusive, intense, insensitive, harsh, dominating, cold

The Dramatic persona finds its ideal expression in leadership roles that demand a commanding presence, unwavering confidence, and the ability to captivate and persuade even the toughest audiences. Whether in high-stakes commercial real estate negotiations, luxury property auctions, or pivotal presentations to investors or municipal authorities, Dramatics excel at owning the room and driving decisions.

In the world of luxury real estate auctions, Dramatic personalities shine as auctioneers or auction house directors. Their authoritative persona and flair for the theatrical create an atmosphere of excitement and exclusivity, driving up bids and closing deals on the most prestigious properties.

Dramatics also excel in real estate investment and finance, particularly in roles that involve high-pressure deal-making, such as in commercial real estate acquisitions, real estate investment banking, or private equity real estate. Their bold and fearless approach inspires confidence in investors and helps push through complex, high-stakes transactions.

In real estate marketing and brand management, Dramatics excel as creative directors or brand managers, crafting compelling narratives and high-impact campaigns that highlight the unique features of properties. Their ability to create a sense of excitement and exclusivity around a property is invaluable.

In real estate sales roles that cater to an elite, discerning clientele, such as in the luxury residential market or high-end commercial properties, Dramatics can be compelling agents. Their commanding presence and ability to create an aura of exclusivity and prestige around a property can be the key to closing the deal with these demanding buyers.

However, Dramatics might struggle in real estate sectors that prioritize a more low-key, consultative approach, or that deal with more price-sensitive, down-to-earth clientele. In roles that require a softer touch, such as in affordable housing initiatives, community-based real estate development, or in dealing with first-time homebuyers or seniors, the Dramatic's intensity and assertiveness may be perceived as overbearing or insensitive to the unique needs and emotional states of these constituents. In these contexts, a more nuanced, empathetic approach may be more effective than the Dramatic's bold, take-charge style.

Did you catch yourself nodding along as you read about one of these secondary personas? Or maybe you saw a bit of yourself in each—the Caregiver's empathy, the Avant-Garde's creativity, the Glamorous' style, and the Dramatic's flair?

But here's the thing—balance is key. While it's great to tap into those secondary personas when the moment calls for it, leaning too heavily into the extremes can lead to serious misperceptions.

Take the Caregiver, for instance. Sure, empathy and warmth are crucial for impactful leadership, but if you're always showing up in flowing attire, with super cute hair and delicate shoes, constantly prioritizing harmony over speaking up, people might start to see you as just a one-dimensional nurturer. They might overlook your assertiveness and strategic thinking skills.

Or how about the Avant-Garde? Their creativity and boundary-pushing nature can be a major asset, but if you're constantly disrupting client meetings with wild ideas, neglecting practicality, and prioritizing bold fashion choices over substance, you risk being pigeonholed as the "out-there" one, overshadowing your other valuable qualities.

And while we all love a bit of shine, if the Glamorous is overdoing it with the hair, makeup, and revealing outfits, people might start to see you as all style and no substance. They might miss the smart, hardworking real estate leader underneath the glitz.

Finally, there's the Dramatic. Sure, they can command attention like no other, but if they're always cranking up the intensity, they risk intimidating clients and hindering collaboration. It's all about striking a balance, knowing when to dial up the drama and when to tone it down.

Here's the truth: there's no such thing as a perfect persona. You're uniquely you, and that's what makes you awesome. The key is to find harmony between your primary and secondary personas, to let your best self shine through while adapting to different real estate contexts. It's about curating your expression to meet the moment, without losing what makes you, well, you.

And should you seek to delve deeper into the fabric of your perceived identity, the end of this book provides a gateway. There, you will find a QR code and a link to a perception persona audit available on my website—a free tool designed to offer insights into which primary or secondary persona you are currently embodying or are perceived as.

Chapter 5
Leaders Look Professional

Strategic Moves to Authority:
Positioning for the End Game.

Chapter 5: Leaders Look Professional

Let's time travel together for a moment back to a time when professional rules were clearly defined and universally understood. An era when professional identity wasn't just a guideline but a strict code of conduct that everyone followed. The rigidity of these rules might seem stifling to us now, but they also offered a clear road map for how to present oneself within a business environment. Nowadays, navigating the shifting sands of what defines "professional" in today's real estate workplace is an intricate dance. Today, the concept of looking professional for real estate leaders is a vibrant tapestry, mirroring the vast expanse of roles from residential to commercial to land sectors and reflecting diverse cultures, generations, and personal styles.

In the past, dress codes were the compass that directed a look of leadership. These sartorial standards were not just about fashion; they were emblems of seriousness, competence, and intent within a professional context. They allowed brokerages and agencies to create a sense of unity and professionalism through a shared visual standard. However, these dress codes have now become historical markers, from which the present-day dynamic fashion ethos has emerged.

Let's briefly revisit them, not as the definitive rule book they once were, but as a history lesson from which today's fluid fashion landscape evolved.

Dress code level one: boardroom attire. Encapsulating formality, boardroom attire was the pinnacle of real estate leaders' wear. Leaders adorned themselves with classic suits in dark, commanding hues, paired with pristine dress shirts. Skirts for women maintained a standard of knee-length, and accessories were selected for subtlety—closed-toe dress shoes, with pantyhose as an indispensable companion for women, irrespective of the season, and jewelry that whispered of status, such as understated watches or cuff links. Hair was often styled in a restrained manner, and makeup for women was applied with a light hand to accentuate a look of natural authority.

Dress code level two: traditional business attire. Traditional business attire offered a broader palette and softer lines. Suits branched into lighter colors and subtle patterns, whereas shirts could bring a pop of color or a delicate print. Skirts for women relaxed slightly in fit, and footwear expanded to include colored dress shoes. Accessories such as ties or scarves could introduce a personal touch, and jewelry might make a bolder statement. Hairstyles softened, and makeup for women could venture beyond the bare essentials to enhance confidence and presence.

Dress code level three: executive casual. Executive casual introduced an even more personal touch. Blazers paired with slacks or skirts provided a blend of authority and approachability, and the use of fabric and color became more diverse. Dress shoes remained the standard, and hair and makeup could echo the wearer's personality, offering a palette for more vivid expression. Accessories, now more pronounced, allowed creativity to shine through.

Dress code level four: mainstream casual. Mainstream casual offered a departure from tradition. Dress shirts gave way to more relaxed button-downs, even embracing short sleeves for a touch of informality.

The color spectrum widened, and patterns became more playful. Footwear could be comfortably chic, reflecting personal style and practicality. Accessories served as a focal point for individuality, and hair could be more freely styled. Makeup for women, in harmony with this casual air, could be more experimental.

Dress code level five: baseline casual. Baseline casual was the embodiment of relaxed professionalism. Denim could be polished enough for a casual real estate office setting, provided it was clean and well-fitted. Tops could be comfortable yet remain tasteful, and shoes could range from loafers to tasteful sneakers, as long as they were well-kept. Hair could be worn in a variety of styles that still conveyed intentionality, and makeup for women could be as understated or as expressive as the overall ensemble allowed. Accessories, although still present, were chosen for comfort and personal expression.

But let's pause now for a moment and consider the present. The rules that once dictated a look of leadership have been blurred by the evolving landscape of the modern real estate workplace. The once rigid frameworks have softened, morphing into a more nuanced spectrum of acceptable workwear for several reasons, as outlined below.

The concept of "casual" in today's workplace is nebulous and subjective. Have you ever found yourself staring at your closet, wondering if you could get away with your favorite jeans for a property showing? While the traditional business dress code was meticulously defined, "casual" remains an elusive term, leading to uncertainty and inconsistency. What one client considers business casual might be seen as too informal by another. This ambiguity challenges real estate leaders to balance comfort with professionalism, developing a keen sense of appropriateness.

Cultural diversity is reshaping dress norms in the real estate workplace. You might have noticed how nowadays each client meeting can bring together a vibrant mix of styles, each reflecting different cultural norms. Each culture brings its own perspective on professional identity, adding complexity to the definition of professional or casual dress. What is considered respectful and appropriate in one culture might be too formal or too casual in another.

Generational views further complicate dress codes. Ever felt a bit out of place at a brokerage event because you felt too formal or too relaxed compared to the others? Each generation brings its own attitudes toward self-expression and conformity. Older generations might prefer traditional looks, whereas younger generations lean toward more relaxed and individualistic styles. Navigating these generational preferences requires flexibility that honors the values of all generations.

Organizations emphasizing diversity, equity, and inclusion are reshaping dress codes. Have you noticed how expectations have become more inclusive in recent years? Recognizing that traditional dress codes can be exclusionary or discriminatory has led to more flexible workwear policies, ensuring that everyone can express their identities more without fear of prejudice or marginalization.

Gender expression is no longer confined to binary norms. Maybe you've seen colleagues who confidently blend traditionally masculine and feminine styles, or perhaps you do this yourself. The binary understanding of gender-specific clothing is giving way to a more fluid perspective. This evolution is reflected in the acceptance of diverse gender expressions through fashion, allowing individuals to dress in ways that align with their true selves rather than conforming to outdated norms.

The internet and social media blur fashion lines, democratizing fashion and trendsetting. Ever bought an outfit you saw on your Instagram feed, only to realize it's probably not appropriate for your open house? Trends that start online quickly make their way into the real estate office, challenging traditional notions of workplace appropriateness.

The pandemic and remote work have fostered informality, reshaping perceptions of professional attire. Remember the pandemic days of video calls in pajamas from the waist down? The shift to remote work introduced a level of informality previously unseen, blurring the lines between home and office.

The rise of flexible working arrangements and the gig economy has blurred work–life boundaries, contributing to a more fluid approach to workwear. Have you ever needed an outfit that's as ready for a business video call as it is for a quick trip to the store? Real estate leaders seek to integrate their personal style with their professional identity, requiring versatility and comfort that still presents well.

Client interactions now demand authenticity, leading to a shift away from the traditional "suited and booted" approach to leadership. Have you found that your clients respond better when you show a bit more of your personal style? A more relatable look can help build trust and rapport with clients. Real estate leaders can now consider more than ever that their look reflects their genuine personality and fosters a sense of connection, rather than adhering to outdated standards of professionalism.

Let's face it, the future of workplace style is anything but static. It's evolving rapidly, driven by a mix of individualism and changing societal norms. Nevertheless, your professional identity still needs to honor the gravitas of your real estate field, but it also has to be flexible enough to meet the demands of the modern world.

Think of it as finding a common visual language that respects the traditions of your profession while embracing the individuality you can now bring into play. Because clearly, gone are the days of rigid dress codes. The contemporary professional landscape is too dynamic for one-size-fits-all rules. Instead, today's real estate leaders need to craft a look of leadership that meets several key functions. Here's what that looks like. It should . . .

- **Bolster your confidence:** Your look should make you feel invincible and confident in your skin, ready to tackle any real estate challenge with the poise of a superhero.

- **Reflect the environment in which you operate:** Whether it's niche nuances, the cultural ethos of your brokerage, or the expectations tied to your role.

- **Consider the clients you will encounter:** Dress not just for the position you hold but also for the individuals you serve and collaborate with.

- **Facilitate versatility:** It's about selecting pieces that can be mixed and matched to suit any client engagement or unexpected encounters you have throughout the day.

- **Demonstrate deliberate choices:** Show that your style is a thoughtful and intentional component of your real estate leader tool kit.

- **Pay attention to details:** Recognize that grooming, accessories, or the right finishing touches are the final steps to an intentional look.

- **Invest in quality over quantity:** If you show that you invest in yourself, clients assume you have the capability to invest in them too.

- **Balance current trends with classic staples:** Ensure your wardrobe remains relevant yet timeless.

- **Know the narrative you want to express:** With each piece reflecting a chapter of your personal identity, aligning your external presentation with your internal values.

- **Complement, rather than overshadow, your intrinsic real estate talents and abilities:** Use pieces to accentuate your look of leadership without causing unnecessary distraction.

- **Allow your presence to take center stage:** With a look that doesn't clamor for attention but instead supports your professional identity.

- **Avoid the pitfall of feeling compelled to mirror traditionally gendered dress expectations:** Assert that competence and authority are not monopolized by any gender identity.

- **Eschew the pressure to conform to gender norms:** Reinforce the idea that your value is not predicated on these norms but on your real estate expertise and contributions.

- **Embrace trial and error as part of the refinement process:** Experiment with new looks and evolve your look of leadership based on feedback and self-reflection.

And lastly, let's rethink a familiar saying, one that you might have heard or even shared yourself: "Dress for the job you want, not the one you have." While there's truth in it, let's broaden our view. Instead of just aiming for the next step, consider your ultimate career goal.

Envision the pinnacle of your real estate career—perhaps it's to become the chief executive officer of a leading brokerage, the head of a commercial real estate investment firm, the director of an industrial real estate development company, or the top executive at a land acquisition and management corporation.

Whatever your end goal, it's vital to begin embodying that role as early as possible to give yourself and others the chance to see the potential in you right now.

Your wardrobe should be a reflection of your ambition and a projection of your potential—the zenith of your aspirations. Each day is an opportunity to illustrate not just where you are or where you want to be next, but where you are determined to be.

Prescribed Uniformity in Action

Ever noticed how uniforms speak volumes without uttering a word? When we encounter a firefighter in their gear, it can evoke feelings of safety and admiration for their bravery, whereas a judge's robes can instantly convey the weight of justice and fairness.

In many professions, uniforms are silent ambassadors, instantly recognizable symbols that communicate volumes. They serve as a bridge between the role, the person wearing them, and those they serve.

Take law enforcement, for example. When you see professionals adorned with badges and regalia, you immediately recognize them as stalwarts of justice and order. Their uniform is a bastion of safety, instantly commanding respect and projecting the power vested in their roles.

Or consider the military. The distinct camouflage or dress uniforms worn by service members signify honor and discipline. The precise insignia, medals, and ribbons communicate rank, experience, and dedication to service, reflecting an unyielding allegiance to national defense and the collective ethos of their units.

In the health care industry, uniforms are a symbol of cleanliness and precision. Whether it's the scrubs of a surgical team or the white coats of medical executives, these garments communicate a commitment to care and a readiness to heal. They represent a shared identity rooted in expertise and empathy, central to the healer's covenant with patients.

In the airline industry, crews wear uniforms that reflect precision and instill confidence in travelers. A pilot's uniform signifies not just their ability to navigate the skies but also their leadership in ensuring passengers' safety and comfort.

On the manufacturing floor, a uniform serves as protective gear and an emblem of the collective industrial effort.

In the automotive industry, it's common to see leaders at dealerships wearing polo shirts, blazers, or pieces branded with the dealership's logo.

I could go on and on. While at the beginning of this chapter you might have thought to yourself, "Uniforms? Is this really still a thing?" Let me assure you, they are omnipresent.

Think of property management staff, where property managers, maintenance personnel, and security staff wear uniforms to present a cohesive and professional image to tenants and visitors. Or consider model home representatives, who wear branded attire to create a consistent and welcoming environment for prospective buyers. Even leasing agents sometimes have to wear a uniform to ensure they present a polished and professional appearance when showing properties to potential tenants.

The relationship between a uniform and the professional wearing it is both intimate and public. It can kindle a sense of belonging and purpose, creating an instant visual connection with the public. And while the scope for personal expression may seem limited, you can still find creative ways to infuse your look of leadership. Small, compliant changes can help to add a personal touch.

Sometimes, your choice of accessories, even within professional boundaries, can make subtle yet impactful distinctions.

Where regulations permit, the flair of a tasteful pin or the understated elegance of a classic watch can highlight your personal style without straying from the required uniformity. A patterned tie or a functional yet stylish belt can serve as a unique identifier; a slight variation in footwear or the style or color of socks can add a discreet touch of personality.

Hair accessories used to secure styles can be both practical and a reflection of your personal taste. Even the modest addition of a name tag or badge designed with a distinctive font or style can serve as a hallmark of individuality, transforming a generic item into something personal and unique.

Your meticulous care of the uniform itself—the sharpness of a crease, the precision of a tuck, the cleanliness and crispness of the fabric—can convey your dedication to your role and attention to detail. These choices, although seemingly minor, can significantly impact how you are perceived and, more importantly, how you perceive yourself within your role. It's in these meticulously maintained details that your individual pride and professionalism truly shine.

Silent Standards and Unwritten Uniforms

If you think the discussion on uniforms doesn't apply to your real estate field, it's time to think again. Every sector of real estate, every brokerage, and every role operates within a set of unspoken expectations—silent standards that make up the unwritten uniform for you as a real estate leader. These standards aren't usually written in guidelines, but they exist in the collective consciousness.

Think about the world of commercial real estate investment. Even without a formal mandate, the uniform often includes conservative suits, crisp shirts, and subtle accessories. Or take a real estate tech startup, where hoodies, T-shirts, and jeans have become the emblematic garb of innovation and disruptive thinking.

In creative real estate marketing roles, the expectation is to embody creativity with eclectic attire and bold color choices that signal a creative mind at work. Real estate educators are expected to strike a balance between being approachable and authoritative, often opting for smart-casual attire that ensures respect while still being relatable to students. Or, in luxury real estate sales, high-end property development, or premium real estate investment trusts, projecting wealth and sophistication is critical. The unspoken uniform borders on "runway luxury"—reflecting the opulent lifestyles those properties embody.

The unifying thread is that each unspoken uniform aims to visually personify professional archetypes and establishes a tribal signaling system everyone can subconsciously read at a glance.

By decoding these silent standards, you can navigate your real estate sector with a more nuanced understanding of these unarticulated yet powerful norms. It's about reading the room, understanding the culture, and dressing in a way that communicates you belong, that you are a credible player in the field, and that you respect the unspoken rules of the game. So, how do you decode what your silent uniform should look like?

First, start with a simple observation. Look around your real estate workplace or sector. Is there a common thread in how leaders dress? You're not aiming to copy anyone, but rather to understand the visual language and the subtle cues that come with it. Notice the colors, fits, patterns, and levels of formality. Pay attention to the details: the type of watches, shoes, hairstyles, and makeup. These subtleties are your road map.

Consider the context of your interactions. When you're in board meetings, what's the dominant style? At networking events, which styles seem to exude success and influence? These observations act as your guideposts. From boardrooms to casual Fridays, each setting has its unwritten rules that, once cracked, can be a powerful tool in your arsenal.

Reflect on your role within the brokerage or agency. What are the expectations—both spoken and unspoken—for someone in your position? How can your look of leadership showcase your professional identity without saying a word?

Then, think about how far you can integrate your personal touch. Once you grasp the silent standards, you can begin bending them subtly. It's about finding the balance between industry expectations and your personal style—the sweet spot where your silent uniform empowers you to feel authentic and confident in your professional skin. Remember, your silent uniform isn't just about fitting in; it's about standing out in the right ways. It's about aligning your external presentation with your career aspirations and the persona you want to project.

Now, let's circle back to our earlier discussion on perception personas, where we highlighted the power of keywords for each of the seven personas—comfort, values, quality, care, creativity, attraction, and power—that anchor our professional identities. You might find that your unwritten uniform speaks to these keywords and the perceived traits they represent. It might explain why you feel seamlessly integrated in some settings, and if not, like a fish out of water in others. This is not about changing your professional identity, it's about fine-tuning by . . .

Balancing personas: Everyone has a primary persona and one or more secondary personas. It's about leveraging this spectrum appropriately. For example, your Caregiver qualities may be front and center when dealing with first-time homebuyers, whereas your secondary Avant-garde traits can shine when innovative marketing strategies are needed. Balancing personas is about the strategic interplay between different facets. It recognizes that a real estate leader isn't one-dimensional—you can be nurturing and innovative, methodical and creative, caring and authoritarian, all at once.

By emphasizing certain traits in specific contexts, you can align your professional identity with your role's expectations while maintaining your unique essence. This alignment allows you to connect with clients and colleagues on multiple levels and in various scenarios.

Borrowing elements: This involves selectively adopting characteristics from other personas when needed. A Glamorous persona might borrow elements from the Cosmopolitan's flair for quality for a high-stakes commercial real estate negotiation, or a Traditionalist could incorporate the Caregiver's warmth for a sensitive residential transaction. Borrowing elements means curating aspects from other personas to complement your dominant traits. This selective synthesis creates a dynamic professional identity that can adapt and thrive across different real estate settings. It's about enriching your personal narrative by integrating diverse qualities that broaden your appeal and enhance your influence. This nuanced approach allows you to be perceived as multifaceted and versatile, showcasing your ability to evolve and respond to various professional challenges.

Quite frankly, you can also choose to disrupt these patterns of unspoken uniforms. History is full of leaders who have shattered expectations and redefined industry norms, becoming icons of success with their unique looks.

Yet, it's essential to recognize these cases are rare—they stand out against a backdrop of more typical narratives. For every convention-defying success story, there are countless others who navigate the intricate dance of expectations and self-expression with more subtlety. The most common pathway to success often involves aligning with established norms while finding small but significant ways to showcase individuality.

Ultimately, the decision is deeply personal. Your real estate career, your professional identity, your style—these are yours to define.

And this isn't about surrendering to the status quo; it's about making informed choices. Because the silent uniform of your real estate sector or role doesn't need to be a straitjacket; it can be a canvas—sometimes for blending in, sometimes for standing out. The art is in knowing when to do which, and the wisdom is in recognizing that the choice is always, unequivocally, yours.

Internal Mandates We Self-Enforce

Yes, you read that right. Many of us are guilty of setting unwritten rules for ourselves, internal guidelines we adhere to—often unconsciously—that shape our professional identity. These self-imposed standards can be as binding as any brokerage dress code, yet they stem not from a company policy but from our own insecurities and the societal expectations we've absorbed over time.

This self-enforcement can manifest in numerous ways, subtly dictating our choices. It's the invisible uniform we design ourselves, woven from the threads of the "shoulds" and "musts" we've collected throughout our personal and professional lives. They are the mental garments made up of beliefs about how we need to appear to be accepted, respected, and successful.

It's time to take a closer look at the expectations some of us have built for ourselves. Let's unfold a few of them below.

Conforming to traditionally masculine dress codes is a notion deeply rooted in the historical context of the workplace. It's not uncommon for women to think thoughts like, "Should I dress more like my male counterparts to be taken seriously?" or "Will I be seen as less authoritative if I don't adopt a masculine style?" These thoughts are understandable, given the long-standing association between masculine attire and power in professional settings. However, this approach is outdated and not recommended.

First, it can suppress your unique identity, compelling you to fit into an aesthetic that may not resonate with your style or the full breadth of your professional capabilities. If traditionally masculine attire feels inauthentic to you, it can affect your confidence and performance. Remember, your clothing is not just fabric; it's psychological armor.

Second, this notion might unintentionally uphold the very gender biases many industries are striving to overcome. It implies that to be a real estate leader, you must downplay attributes that aren't traditionally masculine.

Instead, choose a look that reflects your professional identity and personal style, allowing for a richer expression of leadership. This is not about clothes overshadowing capability; rather, it's about reinforcing that authority and professionalism are defined by your actions and knowledge, not the cut or color of your clothing.

Dressing in an overly gendered manner to emphasize gender identity can be a nuanced issue as well. For some women, this might manifest as a tendency to overdo it—the boldest lip shade, the most dramatic eye look, the perfectly coiffed hair, the form-fitting or revealing outfit, the excessive use of accessories, you name it. In the pursuit of emphasizing their femininity, they may lean toward an overly glamorized appearance that can actually detract from their professional credibility. On the flip side, some men might fall into the trap of believing that paying attention to their appearance is somehow unmasculine. They may shun any form of grooming or avoid anything that could be perceived as "styling" in an attempt to appear more masculine, or they may even neglect basic self-care.

However, just as adopting a predominantly masculine wardrobe can have pitfalls for women, so too can an excessively gendered presentation for women and men. It risks diverting attention from your real estate competence to your appearance, overshadowing your expertise with personal aesthetics.

The silent but potent subtext is that your professional value is intertwined with conventional beauty standards or gender stereotypes, potentially undermining the respect you command based on merit and accomplishments.

While there's power in embracing and expressing your gender identity, it's crucial to find a balance that doesn't tip into excess. The key is striking a harmonious chord between asserting your gender identity and underscoring your professional identity.

Prioritizing others' needs over your own often goes hand in hand with minimizing attention to oneself or personal expenses. It's not unusual to find yourself thinking, "I shouldn't spend too much on my wardrobe when my family needs resources" or "It's selfish to focus on my appearance when there are more important things to worry about."

You may find yourself allocating resources—time, money, and energy—to support and uplift others, even if it means your needs take a backseat. However, this can result in a professional identity, including your wardrobe, that doesn't reflect your status or ambition, thereby affecting how you're perceived. There's a fine line between being resourceful and neglecting or underselling yourself.

Consistently limiting your expenditure on yourself might unwittingly signal you don't value yourself or your role as much as you should. Managing your finances is smart; however, it's also important to recognize that investing in your professional identity is not mere vanity—it's an integral part of your positioning.

The goal is to achieve a balance, where caring for others doesn't come at the expense of neglecting your needs. Recognize that you can be a supportive real estate leader while still honoring your personal and professional requirements. Allow yourself permission to invest in your professional identity to feel confident and capable and reflective of the real estate leader you truly are.

Holding on to the belief that what has worked for years will continue to serve you well can be another pitfall. Perhaps you've caught yourself thinking, "I've always dressed this way, and it's worked so far, so why change now?" or you glanced proudly at the twenty-year-old coat hanging in your wardrobe.

However, others might perceive an unchanging appearance as a reluctance to adapt to new career phases or interpret it as a lack of investment in one's professional growth. In the real estate workplace, where visual cues often communicate ambition and dynamism, an unaltered look could mistakenly signal complacency or lack of innovation.

This isn't about chasing every fleeting trend or dismissing the value of timeless statement pieces. However, when years turn into a decade with the same look, it may be time to acknowledge your sartorial choices are speaking volumes. Periodically updating your professional attire signals you are evolving, attuned to the present, and investing in your real estate career journey. Updating your look of leadership isn't frivolity—it's a strategic refresh, signaling your continued relevance and evolution in your career and beyond.

Struggling with an "age-appropriate" look is a tug-of-war that spans the spectrum of real estate leaders' careers. You may have caught yourself wondering, "Am I dressing too young for my age?" or "Should I dress more conservatively to be taken seriously?" As a real estate leader, you might wrestle with the expectation of dressing in a way that aligns with perceived age norms—being trendy and youthful or reserved and mature. This self-imposed standard can be confining, often leading to a look that feels out of sync with your personal identity.

The challenge lies in transcending these societal dictates that attempt to define what is suitable for various ages within professional contexts. Such constraints can dilute your individuality and signal messages about your capability in the real estate workplace that are misaligned with your actual attributes and contributions.

In crafting your professional identity, the aim should not be to camouflage your age but to celebrate the individual you have become at every stage of your journey. Authenticity in how you present yourself—acknowledging every wrinkle has been earned and every fresh perspective is valuable—can resonate more deeply than any attempt to conform to narrow age expectations.

Feeling the need to dress down or appear less successful to not intimidate or alienate clients is a notion that can inadvertently undermine your authority as a real estate leader. Thoughts like "If I dress too well, will my clients think I'm flashy?" or "Should I dress more casually to seem more relatable to my clients?" might have crossed your mind. This mentality stems from an attempt to foster relatability. However, it risks devaluing your professional expertise.

While approachability is admirable, compromising your professional identity can backfire. Clients may subconsciously interpret an overly casual appearance as a lack of investment in them or the engagement. It signals you aren't representing the premium value your services provide.

You want clients to feel respected and understood, not condescended to. The key is finding the balance of projecting success without appearing unapproachable or out of touch.

Minimizing efforts under the assumption that skills, not appearance, is what truly matters is an understandable perspective for many real estate leaders. Perhaps you've said to yourself, "My work should speak for itself; I don't need to put effort into my appearance" or "I'm too busy focusing on my job to worry about how I look." The intention of prioritizing substance over superficial style is admirable. However, in leadership roles especially, putting minimal effort into your visual presence can unintentionally signal complacency about your professional identity.

While certainly not the prime factor, your self-presentation directly impacts how your leadership abilities are perceived—fairly or not.

Potential doubts can creep in about commitment, judgment, and respect for the role when you appear disheveled.

The reality is that top performance in leadership requires comprehensive and multifaceted efforts, including conscientious self-presentation. It's about projecting pride in oneself and the responsibilities of representing a brokerage or agency with gravitas.

Limiting self-expression in professional settings is a self-limiting belief often rooted in deep-seated cultural, familial, and societal norms. Perhaps you've told yourself, "I shouldn't stand out too much at work" or "This never was appropriate at work, so why now?" This learned behavior, ingrained from an early age, can become a barrier to showcasing the full richness of your professional identity. Authentic self-expression through clothing is a form of nonverbal communication that speaks volumes about your confidence, creativity, and leadership style. It's about striking a balance between respecting workplace decorum and embracing the distinctive qualities that set you apart.

By gently pushing against these inherited boundaries of self-expression, you open the door to a wardrobe that's not just acceptable but also memorable and true to who you are. It's about allowing yourself to shine within the framework of your professional environment, contributing your unique style to the chorus in a way that is harmoniously yours.

Assuming the "perfection" burden is a self-imposed standard where you believe every aspect of your appearance must be flawless. Perhaps you've found yourself obsessing over every detail, thinking "I can't have a single hair out of place" or "My outfit must be absolutely perfect." Rooted in the idea that respect and competence are tied to a faultless image, this belief places immense pressure on you to maintain an impeccable facade at all times. This burden is not just about appearing professional; it's deeply intertwined with a fear of judgment and the desire for acceptance, leading to heightened anxiety and a critical self-view.

However, the quest for perfection is unattainable and obscures the truth that authenticity and relatability are often more compelling than flawlessness. The most respected real estate leaders present themselves as human—capable of embracing their imperfections.

Releasing yourself from the perfection burden doesn't mean abandoning self-care or professionalism; it's about redefining what those concepts mean to you. It's about accepting minor imperfections and recognizing that your value as a real estate leader is not solely contingent on an immaculate appearance.

These self-imposed standards, these "shadow uniforms," are just a few of the barriers we might unconsciously build around ourselves. But let's take a moment to reframe this discussion. Imagine if, instead of being restricted by these invisible rules, you could harness them as a source of strength and clarity. What if, instead of confining your professional identity, you allowed it to evolve, embracing the full spectrum of who you are? It's about breaking free from the self-imposed limitations that may have held you back, recognizing the power you hold to redefine what your professional identity looks like on your own terms.

Consider this: How much more impactful could you be if you fully embraced your professional identity in every professional interaction? What new heights could your career reach if you stopped adhering to outdated norms and instead set your own standards, driven by confidence and clarity?

Dressing Beyond the Code: Situational Awareness

Picture yourself in the eye of a tornado—a place of eerie calm amidst the chaos swirling around you. Inside, you might feel a sense of stability, a confidence in your own identity and purpose. But step outside that center and you're instantly swept up in a maelstrom of shifting expectations and unpredictable situations.

For your professional identity, understanding the nuances of each context is like reading the wind patterns of the tornado. It allows you to navigate spaces with the acumen your role demands, adapting your look of leadership accordingly. This situational awareness communicates your agility and attunement to the subtleties of each situation, ensuring your visual presence contributes positively to the narrative of your leadership. Because just as a tornado's intensity can vary, there will be times when the usual rules of appearance do not apply, and a different approach is called for. Hence, at times, for example, you'll need to . . .

Consider times of crisis or significant organizational change, where real estate leaders may forgo traditional business outfits for something that reflects solidarity with their team and adaptability. In such scenarios it's less about form and more about symbolism. Think of brokerage restructuring or mergers, a major market shift or a critical project phase, or worldwide crises or a natural disaster affecting your local real estate market. In such instances, choosing a look that is practical, durable, and less formal is crucial. These choices, intentional and considerate, signal you're fully engaged and empathetic to the challenges at hand. It's about rolling up your sleeves, both metaphorically and literally, to lead with empathy and readiness—emphasizing that leadership isn't just about directing from above but about being right there with your team.

Accept that practicality can beat professionalism or personal style. Because, in the diverse environments practical considerations often have to influence our look of leadership. As a speaker at a real estate conference under the glaring focus of the stage lights, you're compelled to select clothes that won't clash with the technology around you. Your clothing should be amenable to the microphones, the lights, and the movement across the stage, just as your grooming should be a touch more polished to ensure your expressiveness translates across the room.

Similarly, if you are a leader in commercial real estate, when you step out from your corporate office to visit a construction site, you may need to adapt your look of leadership not just to ensure safety and practicality but to exemplify you understand the circumstances and environment your team members work in. In these situations, your look of leadership is not just about looking the part but about facilitating the part.

Understand you are a real estate leader at all times, not just during business hours. Your omnipresent professional identity means perception is continuous, and the silent dialogue of your look of leadership is always engaged. You need to remember you are a visible symbol of someone in a position of influence of your brokerage, real estate niche, or personal identity 24/7/365.

Even in the absence of your team members, colleagues, or upper management, your look of leadership should always subtly communicate your role and readiness for engagement. This means that from the coffee shop to the plane where a random encounter with a potential client could occur, your wardrobe choices should always bridge the gap between personal downtime and professional readiness.

Guide your team in understanding this concept. Encourage them to consider their visual presence as an extension of their professional identity, no matter the setting. Foster an understanding that there's always a level of consideration in how each team member reflects the shared identity of your brokerage or agency.

Your leadership in this aspect sets the tone, signaling to your team that professional identity is a constant, ingrained in the very fabric of who you are as a professional collective. By guiding your team in these nuances, you reinforce the brand and reputation of your brokerage, strengthening public confidence in both leaders and the brokerage you represent.

In the midst of the swirling winds of modern leadership, situational awareness emerges as a key navigational tool. But it's more than just a tool; it's a mindset, a way of being that separates the real estate leaders who merely survive from those who thrive.

By adapting your look to each unique context, you're not just reacting to change; you're driving it. You're showing leadership isn't about maintaining the status quo, but rather about embracing what's needed here and now.

In the end, your look of leadership is about so much more than clothing or appearance. It's about embodying the essence of who you are and what you stand for. It's about harnessing the power of your presence to inspire, innovate, and lead with unshakable conviction. That's what truly sets real estate leaders apart from the followers: the skill to read any room or situation and the courage to be an adaptable guide, in any situation, in any context, in any storm.

Chapter 6
Leaders Look Respectful

Failing to Respect Yourself Casts Doubt on Your Ability to Respect Others.

Chapter 6:
Leaders Look Respectful

Let's imagine a boomerang gliding through the air, carving a smooth, curved path against the clear sky. As it travels, it spins with a perfect balance and rhythm. At the highest point of its journey, it pauses for a brief moment before starting its return. With steady precision, it heads back to the hand that launched it, drawn by an invisible force. At least, most often. This is the essence of respect in leadership. The respect you give—to yourself, your team, your clients, and your brokerage—is the force that propels your leadership journey forward. And like a boomerang, the respect you give will most likely come back to you, shaping the trajectory of your career and the impact you have. But respect in leadership is not a single, simple thing. It's a multifaceted gem, with each facet reflecting a different aspect of your professional identity. It's in the way you carry yourself, the way you communicate, the way you make decisions. And of course, it's also reflected in the way you present yourself—your look of leadership.

A respectful professional identity starts with self-respect. When you show respect to yourself through your visual presence, you feel more confident and capable. This confidence translates into your actions, decision-making, and overall demeanor. Your respectful presence becomes a silent ambassador, a visible manifestation of self-regard and a sophisticated acknowledgment of the tremendous responsibility you carry as a real estate leader.

Your respectful professional identity sets the tone for your team. Your respectful presence conveys an unspoken commitment to conducting business at the highest professional standards, ensuring serious matters are handled with the necessary gravitas and discernment. When team members see you consistently presenting yourself with respect, they are more likely to follow your lead, embodying the same standards as you.

For clients, your respectful professional identity is a testament to your dedication and reliability. It articulates values and sets a tone for interactions, signaling you are a serious, trustworthy real estate partner. A leader's respectful presence assures clients that their interests are in capable hands, enhancing your credibility and strengthening professional relationships. This trust is crucial in critical negotiations and high-stakes real estate deals, where the confidence clients have in you can determine the success of your transactions.

As a real estate leader, you are the face of your brokerage. Your respectful professional identity reflects the brokerage's values and standards, reinforcing the brand ethos. It demonstrates a commitment to excellence that permeates the brokerage, from the boardroom to the frontline. By embodying the principles of respect, you elevate the brokerage's reputation, making it a preferred partner in the real estate industry.

As a real estate leader, when you broadcast respect for yourself and others through your look of leadership, you establish an uncompromising benchmark. However, just like the journey of a boomerang, respect in leadership is influenced by the one holding it.

It's a Sign of Self-Respect

What's your job title? Wait, I already know. All of my readers have one thing in common—they are all chief executive officers. Surprised? Or disappointed you can't find this title on your business card yet? Let me explain: in my understanding, you are a CEO—the CEO of your professional identity, the CEO of your brand and reputation, the CEO of your real estate career. You have the power to shape it as you wish, or let it slip away. No one is coming to rescue you; it all starts with you. You are the most important element in your journey, so there's no one else you need to respect more than yourself.

Self-respect is about acknowledging your inherent worth without displaying self-importance. It manifests in the meticulous care you take in your appearance, reflecting an inner ethos of precision and attention to detail. Picture a veteran global VP of real estate enterprise leadership whose impeccable power suits demand attention from the C-suite to frontline agents. Or a director of business development at an elite boutique real estate firm, whose refined attire personifies his investment in a respected heritage brand. Their self-respect radiates outward through thoughtful material selections, cohesive sophistication in styling, and a prioritization of impeccable tailoring and grooming. Even the most subtle accessories and accents broadcast their respected leadership and credible authority.

Self-respect is a visual representation of your professional ethos. At its core, cultivating a respectful professional identity means ensuring every detail is curated with precision and philosophical conviction. Every component must integrate seamlessly within the greater story you seek to inspire, underscoring your unwavering self-respect as a real estate guide worthy of being followed.

This "armor" of self-respect isn't rooted in vanity. It's the outward personification of the pride and diligence, earned through years of excellence in leadership's elite battlegrounds.

Self-respect requires relentless dedication but not superfluous extravagance. Dressing with self-respect isn't about flaunting expensive labels or wealth. But let's be practical: investing in your wardrobe is an act of self-valuation. It's a commitment to the mindset that representing yourself, your team, and your brokerage priorities at the highest level is worth the investment—not an indulgent afterthought. It's about allocating resources wisely to secure components that empower you to look and feel like the respected force your office deserves.

Self-respect extends beyond material investments to include time and effort. Relentless dedication to self-respect in your visual presence isn't just about looking good—it's about embodying leadership principles, discipline, and self-worth. It's a visual affirmation of your readiness to lead, inspire, and achieve at the highest levels. This commitment to self-respect ensures you are willing to take the time and make the effort to always be prepared to face challenges with poise and confidence, reinforcing your position as a real estate leader who commands respect and admiration.

Self-respect involves consistency. Consistency in your visual presence, whether in formal client meetings or casual settings, showcases your reliability and steadfastness. It signals you are dependable and unwavering in your professional standards. By presenting yourself consistently, you create a stable and predictable professional identity that others can rely on. This steadfastness enhances your credibility and inspires confidence in those who work with and for you.

Self-respect includes taking care of your physical and mental health. A healthy real estate leader reflects discipline and self-care, crucial aspects of self-respect that contribute to your professional identity and look of leadership. Physical well-being isn't just about aesthetics but about the vitality and energy you bring into every interaction. Maintaining a vibrant and energetic presence enhances your leadership by showcasing your ability to manage and prioritize your health amidst professional demands.

Mental health is equally significant. A calm and composed demeanor reflects inner strength and stability, essential traits for any real estate leader. Prioritizing mental clarity ensures you can navigate challenges with a level head and make confident decisions.

By exuding physical health and mental clarity, you project an image of resilience and reliability that forms a critical part of your professional identity. This translates into a confident and commanding presence, making you a more effective and inspiring real estate leader.

Embracing self-respect transforms not only how others see you but also how you see yourself. It fosters a sense of purpose and fulfillment that transcends external validations. True leadership begins within, and by cultivating self-respect, you unlock the potential to lead with authenticity, inspire with integrity, and achieve with unwavering resolve.

Remember, no one else will come to rescue you. You are the CEO of your professional identity, your brand, and your career. The power to cultivate self-respect is in your hands. Start with yourself and show yourself the respect you deserve. In the end, the greatest testament to your leadership will not be the accolades you receive but the respect you earn, starting with the respect you give yourself.

It Shows You Respect Others

While self-respect is your foundation, as a real estate leader, you do not act in a vacuum. Your influence extends far beyond yourself, shaping the perceptions and experiences of those around you. The way you present yourself is a powerful communication tool that conveys your respect for others. In an instant, it communicates your intentions, impacting how others perceive you and the environment you create.

When you dress with care and intention, you signal to the diverse individuals and communities you engage with that you value their perspectives and honor their contributions. By embodying respect in your visual presence, you set a tone for a culture where everyone feels valued and empowered.

Your look of leadership impacts how your family and friends are perceived. The way you present yourself extends beyond your professional sphere and impacts how those closest to you are perceived. When you maintain a respectful visual presence, you honor the trust and support of those who have been part of your journey. This broader respect reinforces the trust and admiration others have for your family and network, elevating the collective reputation of all connected to you. Your appearance serves as a testament to the values you share with your inner circle, showcasing a commitment to excellence that uplifts everyone associated with you. It demonstrates you are mindful of the impression you make, not just for yourself but for the broader circle you influence.

Your look of leadership is a signal of respect to your team members. Your commitment to maintaining a respectful visual presence signals to your team that you value their contributions and are dedicated to leading by example. This respect fosters a culture of mutual trust and high standards, encouraging team members to mirror you.

By showing you hold yourself to high standards, you set a powerful example, motivating your team to strive for excellence and fostering a cohesive, high-performing environment.

Your look of leadership reflects the values of your brokerage. Every interaction you have, whether internal or external, reflects on the brokerage you represent. By presenting yourself you demonstrate your respect for the brokerage's mission and vision. This commitment to upholding the brokerage's standards enhances its reputation and strengthens its position in the market. Your respect for the brokerage is evident in how you communicate its values and uphold its brand visually, ensuring your professional identity aligns seamlessly with the corporate identity.

Your look of leadership reflects on those who lead you. As a real estate leader, your respectful visual presence is not just a reflection of your personal standards but also of those who lead and mentor you. Your look of leadership sends a powerful message about the values and expectations of upper management—the senior leaders and executives you represent. By maintaining a respectful visual presence, you honor the trust and responsibility bestowed upon you. It demonstrates your alignment with their vision and your dedication to contributing positively to the brokerage's reputation.

Your respectful appearance is a testament to your respect for your field. As a representative of your real estate profession, your appearance should reflect the highest standards of your industry. This respect for your field demonstrates your commitment to its principles and your role in advancing its goals. By upholding these standards, you contribute to the overall credibility and prestige of your real estate profession, setting a benchmark for others to follow.

Your look of leadership signals respect and reliability to your clients. A respectful visual presence shows you value their time and business, fostering trust and building stronger relationships. This respect is not just about looking great but about demonstrating you understand and appreciate the importance of the client's needs and priorities. This approach not only enhances client satisfaction but also shows clients you value their business and are committed to providing exceptional service.

Your look of leadership should honor cultural diversity. As a real estate leader, showing respect for cultural differences in your visual presence demonstrates your commitment to inclusivity. By acknowledging and celebrating cultural diversity, you create an atmosphere where all team members and clients feel valued and respected. This respect is reflected in your willingness to learn about and adapt to different cultural norms and practices. However, this does not mean you have to dress differently based on every culture you encounter, but rather it ensures your look of leadership does not add friction points and respects the diverse backgrounds of those you interact with.

Your look of leadership should respect religious diversity. Recognizing and honoring the diverse religious beliefs and values of others is crucial in today's interconnected world. Your professional appearance should avoid elements that could be perceived as disrespectful to various religious practices and show openness and respect in all of your interactions. By showing respect for these differences, you promote a culture of acceptance and mutual respect. This respect ensures everyone feels valued, regardless of their religious or ethical background. This sensitivity fosters an inclusive real estate workplace where individuals feel free to express their beliefs and values without fear of discrimination.

Your look of leadership should respect generational diversity. The modern real estate workplace is a blend of multiple generations, each bringing distinct perspectives and strengths. Respecting these generational differences in your interactions shows your appreciation for the diverse experiences and insights each generation offers. By presenting yourself in a way that bridges generational gaps, you foster an inclusive environment. This approach leverages the strengths and perspectives of each age group. Your look of leadership should demonstrate a respect for all generations, ensuring you are approachable and relatable to everyone, regardless of age.

Your professional identity should embrace gender diversity. As societal understanding of gender evolves, it's important to respect and acknowledge diverse gender identities in your professional appearance. This respect not only supports those who identify outside of traditional gender norms but also sets a precedent for acceptance and equality in the workplace. It reinforces your commitment to creating a space where everyone can thrive, free from discrimination or bias. By presenting yourself in a way that acknowledges and respects diverse gender identities, you foster an inclusive environment where everyone feels valued and respected and ensure that your look of leadership avoids reinforcing outdated gender norms and instead promotes a culture of inclusivity and respect.

The way you present yourself as a real estate leader is a profound act of respect that goes beyond superficial appearances. It is an affirmation of your commitment to the values and principles that underpin your professional and personal interactions. By consciously cultivating a look of leadership that honors the diverse identities and backgrounds of those you engage with, you create a powerful ripple effect that fosters inclusivity, trust, and collaboration.

This dedication to respectful self-presentation not only enhances your credibility and influence but also serves as a beacon of inspiration for others to follow. As you navigate the complexities of modern leadership, let your appearance be a testament to your unwavering respect for the humanity and dignity of every individual you encounter. This approach will not only elevate your own leadership journey but also contribute to building a more compassionate and connected professional world.

It's Not Always Reciprocated

Remember the boomerang we launched at the beginning of this chapter? Ideally, it gracefully returns to your hand, but as we all know, that isn't always the case. Whose fault is it when the boomerang doesn't come back? Is it the fault of the thrower, the craftsmanship of the boomerang, the whims of the wind, or the conditions surrounding it? The answer often remains elusive.

And the same is true for respect. While we all hope it would be reciprocated, this is not always the case.

It might be your team member who shows up disheveled at your client meeting, your own upper management who don't represent the brokerage in the way they should, or a colleague whose lack of professionalism undermines the team's efforts. As a real estate leader who meticulously cultivates a respectful professional identity, it can be disheartening to encounter individuals who do not extend the same courtesy.

Understanding why this happens and how to navigate these challenges without compromising your own standards is essential for sustaining your integrity and leadership. While we might have an idea why that boomerang didn't return, there are plenty of reasons why others may not reciprocate the respect you consistently demonstrate, as outlined below.

Lack of Awareness: Some real estate professionals may simply be unaware of the importance of maintaining a respectful appearance in professional settings. They might not recognize how their visual appearance affects others or understand the impact of a respectful look of leadership. This lack of awareness can lead to unintentional disrespect, stemming from ignorance rather than malice. It's essential to understand these individuals might not be acting out of ill will but rather from a place of unfamiliarity with professional standards.

Different Standards: Unfortunately, not everyone adheres to the same standards of visual appearance. Some real estate professionals may prioritize their own interests above mutual respect, displaying a lack of consideration in their appearance that is self-serving or inconsiderate. Such actions undermine the collective effort and can create an atmosphere of resentment. As a real estate leader, it is crucial to set and uphold high standards and reinforce the importance of a respectful and professional appearance in achieving shared goals.

Personal Context: You never know their full story. It's important to remember everyone has a unique story and context that may not be immediately visible. Personal struggles, health issues, cultural differences, and challenging circumstances can all influence how someone presents themselves. You must be careful not to jump to conclusions or make assumptions about someone's lack of respect based solely on their appearance. Instead, approach these situations with empathy and understanding, recognizing there may be unseen factors at play.

External Pressures: Pressures, such as tight deadlines, emergencies, or high-stress situations, can impact how real estate professionals present themselves. These pressures might lead to moments where maintaining a respectful appearance is not a priority. While you can show understanding for these temporary lapses, it's important to recognize they can only be temporary.

Personal Insecurities: Real estate professionals who are insecure about their own appearance may exhibit disrespectful actions as a defensive mechanism. They might feel threatened by your look of leadership, leading them to undermine or dismiss your efforts in an attempt to bolster their own self-esteem. Understanding that such behavior often stems from a place of insecurity allows you to address it with empathy rather than frustration.

Economic Constraints: Not everyone has the same financial resources to invest in a professional wardrobe appropriate for real estate. Economic constraints can affect how real estate professionals present themselves, leading to differences in appearance that might be mistaken for a lack of respect. Although financial limitations are difficult for you to change as a real estate leader, it's important to create an understanding that a respectful visual appearance doesn't mean you have to break the bank.

Environmental Influences: Real estate professionals might adopt a more casual or disheveled appearance because they see it modeled by others. This can create a vicious cycle where a lack of attention to visual appearance becomes normalized, thereby eroding respect. As a real estate leader, it is vital to recognize the impact of the organizational culture on look of leadership and work proactively to cultivate a more respectful environment. This includes setting clear expectations for appearance, modeling a respectful look of leadership, and addressing issues of neglect promptly and effectively.

Rebellion Against Norms: Like it or not, some real estate professionals might intentionally reject conventional standards of respectful appearance as a form of personal expression or rebellion against what they perceive as outdated norms. This can be their conscious choice to challenge the status quo and advocate for a more relaxed or inclusive definition of professionalism.

There's really not much you can do other than respecting their choice and maintaining your own standards. If they are in your sphere of influence, you can continue to mentor them or unfortunately have to consider if they are the right person for your team.

Maintaining your own standards of respect, even when it is not reciprocated, is an act of resilience and integrity. It is a testament to your real estate character and commitment to leadership excellence. This steadfast adherence to your values, even in the face of nonreciprocity, sets you apart as a true real estate leader. Respect is not merely an exchange but a reflection of your inner ethos. It's a gift to yourself and those you lead, regardless of how it is reciprocated. So, never let go of your own standards, no matter how much you are tested.

Damage Control: When Things Go Wrong

Have you ever thrown a boomerang and watched it veer off course, causing a moment of panic? Perhaps it narrowly missed someone's face, or worse, actually struck them. It's a stark reminder that even with the best intentions, things can go wrong. And just like with a boomerang, our actions in the professional world can sometimes have unintended consequences.

The spectrum of potential missteps is vast. It can range from minor slipups, such as arriving a few minutes late to a team meeting or forgetting to silence your phone during a listing presentation, to more significant blunders, such as making an insensitive comment or a well-intended joke that falls flat.

In extreme cases, a severe lapse in judgment or a major ethical violation could even escalate into a full-blown crisis, potentially attracting media attention and putting the reputation of your entire brokerage at risk.

Regardless of the scale, when our professional identity takes a hit, the damage can be profound.

It's not just about a momentary embarrassment or inconvenience; it's about the long-term erosion of trust, credibility, and respect we've worked so hard to build.

So, you've made a mistake, and now you're facing the daunting task of damage control. How do you navigate this delicate situation and start rebuilding those vital bridges of trust and respect in the real estate world? First and foremost, avoid the following two common pitfalls:

Ignoring the problem and hoping it will go away. You might feel like you're not responsible for how others feel and therefore choose to simply ignore the issue and move on. However, by doing so, you're losing control over the situation and its outcome. You can't be sure if the other party will move on, forget about it, forgive you, or share with others how you supposedly made them feel. Remember, your professional identity is not just what people tell you to your face; it's what they say about you behind your back. If you don't take control of your professional identity, others will shape it for you. The tension between your belief that an apology isn't necessary and others thinking you don't own your mistakes can create a toxic real estate work environment.

A hollow apology is just as bad as no apology. The second mistake often made, particularly if you don't feel entirely responsible for what happened, is to blurt out a quick "sorry" when the other party might expect a more genuine apology. This can make them dislike or distrust you even more because it suggests you haven't taken the issue seriously enough. If you believe an apology is in order, it's crucial to deliver it with sincerity and thoughtfulness.

So, let's take a closer look at how a proper apology should be executed.

Begin with self-forgiveness. This might sound trivial, but it's a crucial first step. Forgive yourself. Everyone makes mistakes, and everyone has "off" days. You've likely had to apologize for something at some point in your real estate career. The key is to do your best every day. How you go about making things right and growing from your faults says more about you as a real estate leader than your original mistake.

Assess the impact. Once you've let go of the self-judgment that's holding you back, do your homework. Analyze the situation and try to understand how the other party may feel. Ask yourself tough questions about what exactly went wrong, the consequences, and how it could have been handled better. This will help you grasp the details of the misstep and enable you to craft an apology that goes beyond a simple "sorry."

Choose the right timing. The timing of your apology is crucial and can vary depending on the severity of the mistake. For minor errors, such as arriving late to a client meeting, an apology is expected and accepted quickly. However, for more significant blunders, you might need to wait a few hours or even a day until emotions have settled and everyone involved is ready to process the situation and accept an apology.

Opt for one-to-one conversations. When planning your apology, keep in mind this conversation should happen privately, in a one-to-one setting. If your apology involves sensitive topics such as sexual misconduct, alcohol or drug abuse, or religious issues, it's best to immediately seek guidance from your HR department or legal counsel. In most other cases, always aim for a private conversation with the person you need to apologize to. Later, you can involve your boss or others if needed and share that you've worked things out.

Avoid technology if you can, prioritize face-to-face interaction. Whenever possible, apologize in person. A face-to-face conversation is always better than communicating via text message, email, chat, or even a phone call. When you apologize in person, you allow the other individual to hear your voice and see your facial expressions, and vice versa. If you send a quick "sorry" message, you can't gauge their reaction. You hit "send" and lose control over the process. If an in-person apology isn't possible, a video call is likely your next best option. Keep in mind your nonverbal cues are important, whether in person or on a webcam. And also keep in mind that nowadays everything can be recorded.

"I am sorry." Say it out loud, and mean it. Your apology will only sound authentic if you truly are sorry. This is the first step to regaining trust and accepting forgiveness. Take responsibility for your actions and claim the blame. Say, "I realize I made a mistake" or "I understand you were hurt." Own the errors you made without shifting blame onto someone or something else in an attempt to reduce responsibility.

Avoid getting defensive or making excuses. While it might be tempting to overexplain your actions, trying to justify why you thought your behavior was acceptable can make others feel like you still don't understand the problem. Simply admit what went wrong, showing that you're not operating from your ego.

Share your lessons learned. After acknowledging your mistake, share what you've learned and how you plan to act differently in the future. Offer to resolve the issue or fix the error if possible. If you can't do so this time because what's done is done, explain how you'll prevent similar situations from happening again. Ensure you're able to follow through on your commitments and never repeat the inappropriate behavior. People are often very forgiving once, but it will be harder for you to recover if you make the same or a similar mistake again.

Listen more than you speak. Once you've said your piece, stop talking and listen. Allow others to respond to your apology and express their disappointment, feelings, or perspective on the situation. Resist the urge to become defensive or justify your behavior in response to their comments.

Express your gratitude. To close the conversation and move forward, offer a simple thank-you. Don't overdo it; just express your appreciation for the opportunity to address and discuss the issue, then move on. Dwelling on the same problem and rehashing the same reasoning repeatedly can cause the negative experience to become more entrenched in both your minds.

Be patient in rebuilding trust. Perhaps the most challenging step for many is patience. Regaining others' trust in the real estate world requires patience, perseverance, and, most importantly, time. It's unreasonable to expect others to immediately trust you again. Give them the time they need, otherwise you risk undermining the entire process. Eventually, you must let go of the experience. This encounter doesn't define you and will often linger in your thoughts longer than it stays with others.

Throughout the process, transparency, humility, and a genuine commitment to change are key. Leaders must be willing to have difficult conversations, to listen to feedback, and to put in the hard work of rebuilding trust. It's not easy, and it's certainly not comfortable. But handling mistakes with grace, accountability, and a focus on repair is a hallmark of strong leadership. It shows you're human, yes, but also that you're committed to growth, integrity, and the well-being of those you lead. In the end, your professional identity is not defined by your mistakes but by how you respond to them. So the next time your boomerang goes a little astray, remember, it's not about the stumble but about the recovery. It's about picking up that boomerang, learning from the throw, and stepping up to try again.

Chapter 7
Leaders Look Controlled

The More You Control,
the Better the Outcome.

Chapter 7: Leaders Look Controlled

As a captain of a ship you navigate through the vast, unpredictable ocean. Every decision you make, every course you chart, and every adjustment to the sails is critical. The ocean is full of challenges—unseen currents, sudden storms, and hidden reefs. Yet, your ability to maintain control determines the success of your voyage. You must be constantly aware of your surroundings, vigilant about the state of your vessel, and ready to steer your ship through whatever comes your way. Similarly, maintaining control over your professional identity is paramount. Each piece must be positioned with intention. Every choice should be a deliberate act. Every detail declares the control you possess over your narrative. It's a powerful statement that says, "I steer the course of my real estate identity," and it speaks volumes about your self-assurance and the respect you command—silently yet resoundingly.

Although not every perception can be influenced, neglecting to craft your professional identity consciously allows others to fill in the blanks, often with incongruent strokes. By intentionally shaping your narrative, you ensure it remains firmly in your hands, a true reflection of your ability to guide not only your path but also the trajectory of those who follow your real estate lead.

Taking control of your professional identity is not an act of vanity but a strategic move. It's an affirmation that even though you can't control every perception, you can certainly lay a solid, indelible foundation that resonates with the identity you aim to project.

Why leave such a powerful thing to chance? Why permit happenstance to dictate what can be shaped with purpose and precision?

Like a skilled CEO who strategizes and executes each business move with precision and foresight, as a real estate leader, you must embrace every tool at your disposal. Your real estate career is a tapestry of roles and achievements, but also of the conscious effort to sculpt your professional identity with intention. This process includes the following:

- **Self-awareness:** where reflection becomes as routine as strategy meetings;

- **Self-care:** where discipline in personal presentation is akin to financial stewardship; and

- **Self-promotion:** where advocating for your achievements is as crucial as marketing your brokerage's successes.

By cultivating your professional identity with such intention and control, you do more than advance your real estate career trajectory—you lay down a pathway for excellence.

Self-Awareness and Self-Reflection: Controlling Your Inner Compass

How often do you wonder if your professional identity aligns with the perception others have of you? It's a critical question that every real estate leader should ask themselves—continuously. Understanding how you are perceived by your team members, colleagues, upper management, and clients can make a significant difference in your leadership effectiveness.

This reflection isn't just about seeing your strengths; it's also about acknowledging your weaknesses and biases.

By continuously questioning and evaluating your actions and motives, you can ensure your professional identity truly represents who you are and what you stand for. This journey of self-awareness and self-reflection is about taking control of your inner compass, guiding your professional path with intention.

Controlling your self-awareness means continually looking inward, asking tough questions about your motives, your own biases, and the impact of your decisions. It involves taking a moment after each significant event to evaluate what went right and what didn't.

But self-awareness goes beyond just personal reflection. It's about understanding how your professional identity influences your brokerage's culture, recognizing the pivotal role you play in your team and how your professional identity affects team cohesion.

This self-awareness should shape your look of leadership, guiding you to cultivate a visual presence that aligns with your role and the expectations of those who look up to you. Considering your look of leadership isn't superficial—it's strategic. It's about how your visual presence can reinforce or undermine perceptions of your competence, approachability, and professionalism.

Constantly ask yourself: "Does my wardrobe convey the authority and expertise expected of my real estate role?" "Is my look accessible and reassuring to clients from diverse backgrounds?" or "How does my style affect my team's perception of my leadership?"

As a real estate leader, your visual presence should answer these questions and reflect your core principles. It's about choosing clothing that not only fits you but also fits the moment and the mission.

Self-Care and Self-Discipline: Controlling Your Well-Being

Have you ever struggled to find the balance between taking care of yourself and leading others? Trust me. You are not alone. It's a common challenge that many real estate leaders face. The demands of leadership can often overshadow the need for self-care, but neglecting your own well-being can have serious repercussions. Think about the last time you felt exhausted or overwhelmed—how did it affect your ability to lead effectively?

Just like on an airplane where you're told to put your own oxygen mask on before helping others, self-care follows the same principle: if you neglect your own well-being, it will affect your ability to lead. To be seen as capable of nurturing and guiding others, you must visibly take care of yourself first.

This isn't about being indulgent but about fundamental maintenance that enables effective leadership. It signals to others you are well-prepared to manage the multifaceted demands of leadership. It shows you understand the importance of balance and are equipped to handle the various responsibilities and individuals who rely on your guidance and expertise.

Discipline is the commitment to maintaining these self-care practices regularly and making choices that align with your long-term real estate goals, even when they require sacrifice or delayed gratification. This includes habits such as getting enough sleep, eating nutritious food, staying physically active, and practicing mindfulness. These activities are not luxuries but necessities that enable you to perform at your peak.

Discipline, especially in self-care, also means setting boundaries to protect your time and energy. It involves saying no to nonessential demands and recognizing when you need to step back and recharge.

For many real estate leaders, there's an imbalance where the rigor applied to caring for others isn't always matched by the discipline needed for self-care.

Acknowledging and addressing this imbalance is crucial because disciplined self-care is the reservoir from which the strength to lead others is drawn. Applying the same level of discipline to your well-being as you do to your professional duties is essential for your professional identity.

Self-Improvement and Self-Promotion: Controlling Your Narrative

Have you ever felt hesitant to promote your achievements for fear of being seen as boastful? It's a delicate balance that many real estate leaders struggle with. On the one hand, you want to highlight your successes and the value you bring to your brokerage. On the other hand, you fear coming across as arrogant or self-serving. But consider this: if you don't advocate for your achievements, who will?

Effective self-promotion is not about bragging; it's about controlling your narrative and ensuring your contributions are recognized and valued. It's about owning your story and using it to pave the way for future successes. Remember, as the CEO of your own real estate career, you control these aspects to ensure your professional identity and visual presence remain strong and dynamic—and that they are known, seen, and heard.

It's about articulating and celebrating your achievements not out of vanity but as advocacy for the value you bring to your brokerage. This approach paves the way for your advancement and raises the profile of your team's efforts, aligning with and advancing collective real estate objectives.

Still, many grapple with the fine line between being perceived as confident and being labeled as self-important. Concerns about backlash or being seen as not team-oriented add to this complexity, which in turn is compounded by imposter syndrome where high achievers fear being exposed as frauds. Cultural factors also play a role; in some cultures, self-promotion is seen as boasting.

This belief can influence real estate leaders' willingness to engage in self-promotion. Despite these obstacles, self-promotion is critical for your professional identity.

Self-improvement, however, often easily translates into a relentless pursuit of perfection. There's an ingrained belief that to succeed, one must not only match but exceed standards set by predecessors or counterparts—every single time. This drive, although admirable, can morph into an endless quest where "good enough" rarely is, and the goalposts of achievement keep moving.

This pressure to continuously improve and strive for flawlessness creates an exhausting cycle of self-imposed expectations. The journey to your professional identity should be reframed from a race toward unattainable perfection to a journey of growth that values progress over perfection. It's about recognizing the merit in each step of your development, celebrating small victories and understanding that making mistakes is a natural part of learning.

Always remember: your approach to these topics directly influences your professional identity. Your look of leadership isn't just about the clothes you wear; it embodies the confidence with which you share your accomplishments and the grace with which you pursue development. It's in the assured way you carry yourself, knowing you've earned your place, and in the mindful choices that reflect a commitment to continuous improvement. It's about the care you put into yourself and the awareness that you deserve it.

You—and only you—are in control of your professional identity. Your look of leadership is a visible extension of your journey. Let it be an armor of empowerment, woven with threads of your professional narrative. This look—your look—of leadership isn't static. It evolves as you do, shaped by the choices that position you as an expert and the controlled steps of development that keep you dynamic and forward-thinking. It's a look that respects where you've been and anticipates where you'll go, all while asserting the undeniable impact you make every single day.

Be Prepared for the Predictable and the Unpredictable

Are you a planner? Maybe even a micromanager? I admit, I like to have control—I like knowing what's ahead. I like having a plan. There's a certain comfort in feeling prepared, in anticipating every move and scenario. It's the reassurance that comes from having a road map, a clear path forward.

But, let's be honest—how often does everything go exactly as planned in the real estate world? How often do we find ourselves navigating uncharted waters, dealing with unexpected challenges that no amount of planning could foresee?

In leadership, this tension between the known and the unknown is a constant. The ability to face both the predictable and the unpredictable becomes a defining trait of effective leadership. As you stand at the nexus of daily challenges and dynamic shifts, the ability to anticipate and adapt is essential. Hence, your look of leadership should be curated not just for aesthetic appeal but for its strategic function. Curating it with intention is an exercise in scenario planning, a rehearsal for the diverse roles you play to align the tangible elements of your look of leadership with the intangible dynamics of your day.

Embarking on this sartorial strategy requires contemplation—a series of reflective questions that may guide your choices and ensure your look of leadership is congruent with your professional objectives. Consider, for example, the following questions:

- What's the big picture for today?
- What's the occasion?
- With whom will you be interacting?
- What will your clients be wearing?
- What will your upper management be wearing?
- What will your colleagues be wearing?
- What will your team members be wearing?
- Where are you going to meet?
- Where are you possibly heading after you've met?

- How will you get there?
- Who else could you randomly meet today?
- What message do you have to deliver today?
- What real estate scenarios will you be facing today?
- Are there cultural considerations or social norms to account for?
- How might your schedule or travel impact your ability to refresh your look?
- Will you potentially be recorded on video or photographed?
- How does your look honor the real estate narrative you wish to convey?
- How does your look serve as a model for others in your real estate niche?
- How can your attire make a statement about the inclusivity and diversity you champion in the real estate industry?

The answers to these questions (and possibly many more) form the cornerstone of your professional presentation. They guide you to select a look that not only matches the situations you'll face but also allows you to shine a light on those you weren't otherwise prepared for. By strategically planning, you're taking command of an element of your professional identity that's too often left to happenstance. It's an intentional choice, the armor of a real estate leader poised to tackle the day's challenges.

It's Not Only about Clothes

Looking the part is merely the opening act. While a professional appearance can open doors and instill confidence, it's the substance behind the style that truly defines a real estate leader. A leader's visual presence is undeniably important, but it must go hand in hand with their behavior, communication, digital footprint, and environment.

These elements work together to create a comprehensive professional identity that resonates with team members and reinforces a leader's impact. So, let's revisit once again, as a reminder, the other factors that are crucial for your professional identity.

BEHAVIOR: Your behavior carries as much weight as your appearance in shaping both your team's and clients' perceptions of your leadership. The way you conduct yourself—your actions, reactions, and interactions—becomes a living testament to your professional identity. In the daily demands of leadership, where challenges and opportunities often coincide, your behavior serves as a guiding light for your team members and sets the tone for client interactions. It should embody the virtues your look of leadership suggests.

Consider this: you may dress impeccably, with every detail curated to convey authority, but if your behavior does not align with this presentation, your appearance becomes an empty shell. This disconnect not only confuses your team but also sends mixed signals to clients, potentially undermining their confidence in your capabilities.

Your composed conduct amidst adversity, clear directives, and swift decision-making reflect the respect and control suggested by your professional appearance. You must be the steady presence in times of tumult, the clarity in times of uncertainty, and the empathy in every strategic decision you make. This consistency reassures your team and builds trust with your clients, reinforcing your reliability and professionalism.

If you present yourself as a confident, decisive real estate leader through your visual presence but exhibit indecisiveness, lack of composure, or poor judgment in your actions, the disconnect between your appearance and behavior can erode your team's trust and respect, as well as your clients' trust in your ability to deliver results. However, if your behavior consistently aligns with the qualities suggested by your appearance, it reinforces your credibility as a real estate leader and solidifies client relationships.

This influences not just how your team perceives you but also how willingly they follow your real estate lead and embrace open communication and collaboration. Similarly, it impacts how clients perceive your professionalism and reliability, affecting their willingness to engage with and commit to your services. The tone you set through your behavior impacts everything from team morale to performance standards and client satisfaction.

Let your behavior complement your look of leadership, not contradict it.

COMMUNICATION: Effective communication in leadership is a nuanced art. It's not merely what you say; it's how you say it. Your tone, choice of words, and clarity in expressing your thoughts can alleviate stress or, if mishandled, exacerbate it. Your visual appearance opens the door, but your communication invites team members and clients in, offering them a seat at the table.

Imagine you're presenting at a team meeting. Your crisp look of leadership sets a professional tone, but it's your persuasive communication that will be remembered. You choose words that inspire, not just inform. You explain; you don't just direct. You listen—truly listen—not only to respond but also to understand and connect. This approach not only motivates your team but also reassures clients of your dedication and understanding. In these critical moments, your ability to communicate with compassion and clarity can make the difference in how your professional identity is perceived. Your communication is the audible manifestation of your look of leadership. When in harmony with your appearance, it establishes you as a real estate leader who is not only seen but heard and understood by both your team and your clients.

However, if your communication is unclear, contradictory, or lacks empathy, it can negate the positive impression created by your visual presence. If you look the part of a confident, articulate real estate leader but struggle to communicate effectively, the disparity can undermine your team's confidence in your abilities and cause clients to question your reliability.

However, if your communication skills consistently match the message conveyed by your appearance, it amplifies your impact as a real estate leader. Your words and your look work in harmony, making your leadership more persuasive and influential.

DIGITAL FOOTPRINT: Your digital presence is a reflection of your reputation, real estate expertise, and judgment. This digital reflection of you can either strengthen your team's and clients' trust in your professional capabilities or raise doubts about your fitness as a real estate leader.

As you navigate the complexities of your digital presence, consider the emotional contexts in which your digital presence might be scrutinized. Your digital footprint is not limited to traditional working hours—at any time, 24/7/365, others make assumptions about your professional identity by the digital breadcrumbs you leave behind. Even while you're leading a real estate meeting, team members or clients might be looking you up online, possibly right there in the room or during a break. They might come across your digital interactions, shaping their emotional response before they even engage with you directly.

Your digital professional identity should not merely be a shadow of your in-person identity; it should be its affirmation. Ensure consistency between your digital presence and your physical presence to fortify your professional narrative. This congruence reassures and confirms to your team and clients that the real estate leader they encounter online is the same one leading the charge in the office or in the field.

If your digital presence is inconsistent with the professional image you present in person, it can create cognitive dissonance for your team members and clients. For example, if you maintain a polished, professional appearance in the real estate office but your online presence is filled with unprofessional content, inflammatory remarks, or inconsistencies, it can lead your team and clients to question your judgment, integrity, and reliability.

Hence, aligning your digital presence with your look of leadership is crucial. It demonstrates consistency, authenticity, and a commitment to professionalism across all channels. When your digital footprint mirrors your professional appearance, it strengthens your team's and clients' trust and respect for your leadership.

ENVIRONMENT: The choices you make, from the car you drive to the books on your office shelves, contribute to the tapestry of your professional identity. Each decision, even if seemingly unrelated to your professional responsibilities, can color your team's and clients' perceptions of you.

Consider, for instance, the vehicle you choose; it's not merely a means of transportation but a reflection of you. A poorly maintained car might inadvertently convey to team members and clients a disregard for modern efficiency. Conversely, a luxury sports car might lead to assumptions of extravagance, which could cause them to question your financial judgment.

The layout and condition of your office project your style. An organized, aesthetically pleasing, and functional workspace not only enhances your productivity but also sends a clear message of professionalism and attention to detail—qualities revered in any leadership role. This impression extends to clients who visit your office, reinforcing their trust in your capabilities.

Think also of the individuals you associate with—friends, family, colleagues. Their appearance, behavior, communication, and digital presence can reflect on you, too, positively or negatively. You are judged by the company you keep, so it's prudent to surround yourself with individuals who support and amplify your professional identity. This holds true not only for your team but also for clients who observe your professional network.

If your environment is at odds with the professional identity you want to be known for, it can create a jarring disconnect for your team and clients. When your surroundings, associations, and choices align with the qualities reflected in your visual presence, it creates a cohesive, trustworthy impression.

It shows your commitment to professionalism is not just superficial but deeply ingrained in every facet of your life, instilling confidence in both your team and your clients.

Every aspect of your professional identity contributes to the overarching narrative of who you are as a real estate leader and how your team or clients perceive you. Inconsistencies between your look of leadership and your behavior, communication, digital presence, or environment can undermine your credibility and effectiveness. By ensuring alignment and consistency across all these elements, you strengthen your professional identity, build trust with your team, and amplify your impact as a real estate leader. The situations you navigate may differ, but the emotional undercurrents of judgment and perception are universal, influencing how you are seen and understood in your leadership role.

Chapter 8
Leadership in a Digital Landscape

The More You Share, the More They Discover.
The Less You Share, the More Suspicion You Invite.

Chapter 8:
Leadership in a Digital Landscape

Gone are the days when the measure of a real estate leader was taken first and foremost through a firm handshake or a direct look in the eye. Today, it's the digital handshake—be it a LinkedIn profile, a professional bio on a brokerage website, a glance through a webcam, or an introductory email—that often precedes any physical meeting. This digital first encounter can be influential enough to impact decisions and perceptions long before a face-to-face interaction. The digital portrait of a real estate leader must now be as meticulously crafted as one's physical presentation. A hastily composed profile, a poorly chosen profile picture, or an unprofessional post can significantly impact one's professional reputation. Nowadays, search engines act as the new background check, and your online identity speaks volumes, setting the stage for all future interactions. It's your digital breadcrumb trail that leads others to your professional doorstep—or doesn't. It forms the narrative of who you are, what you represent, and how you conduct your professional life. A well-managed digital presence can open doors and establish a narrative of real estate expertise and trustworthiness. Neglect it, and you may find that the narrative is written without your consent, shaped by others' interpretations and the whims of algorithms.

The stakes are high. Your digital presence has the power to bolster or undermine the hard-earned emblems of your professional identity.

As such, it's imperative you not only adapt to this digital evolution but also embrace it with the same level of precision and dedication you apply to any professional endeavor.

- **Internal impact:** Your digital footprint carries significant weight in shaping how you are perceived by your team and colleagues within the brokerage. A robust digital presence that showcases your best self can inspire confidence and respect among your team members. It sets a benchmark for professional standards within your team. Conversely, a neglected or inconsistent digital profile may lead to doubts about your leadership relevancy and adaptability in a tech-driven world.

- **External impact:** Externally, your digital footprint serves as a critical touchpoint for clients assessing your credibility and real estate expertise. A well-curated digital presence that aligns with your professional acumen can significantly sway client decisions and enhance trust in your leadership. It shapes how potential partners view your reliability and forward-thinking nature. In the decision-making process, clients often seek reassurance not just through direct interactions but also by examining the digital personas of the real estate leaders they choose to engage with. Thus, your digital engagements and the narratives they build play a pivotal role in determining business opportunities and partnerships.

Your digital footprint is a complex tapestry woven from two distinct threads: the intentional and the unintentional. The intentional footprint is the result of your deliberate actions and choices online, whereas the unintentional footprint is shaped by the subtle cues and signals your digital presence emits. Understanding and managing both aspects is crucial for crafting a cohesive and compelling online narrative.

Your intentional footprint: Every click, post, and interaction within your digital landscape is a brushstroke in the portrait of your professional identity. This intentional footprint is about crafting a narrative that resonates with your leadership style and professional goals. It includes the content you create, the networks you engage with, and the professional conduct you maintain online. These deliberate actions are your direct voice in the digital world, offering a narrative that speaks of your real estate expertise, your professional journey, and your thought leadership.

Pause and reflect on the intentional echoes your online actions create. In the digital world, every click, post, and email contributes to the intentional aspect of your digital footprint. This footprint is a carefully crafted mosaic, each piece a deliberate action adding up to the sum of your online presence. The photograph you choose for professional networking sites, the insightful articles you publish on industry trends, the supportive comments you leave on forums—these are the brushstrokes of your intentional digital presence.

Your unintentional footprint: Contrary to the controlled narrative of the intentional footprint, the unintentional footprint consists of the passive signals your digital presence emits. These might include how frequently you update your professional profiles or the timeliness of your responses. This digital body language can also subtly influence perceptions of your professional identity. Just like body language in personal interactions, these digital cues provide a backdrop against which your explicit actions are measured. They whisper tales of your dedication to staying current and responsive in a swiftly evolving digital real estate era.

The state of your professional profiles also whispers secrets about your attention to detail and relevance in a rapidly evolving professional landscape. A profile with outdated information or with broken links can inadvertently suggest a disconnection. Your tech-savviness—or lack thereof—is apparent in the way you navigate digital tools and platforms.

Do you leverage the latest features, or do you falter with the basics of digital communication? And let's not forget the omnipotent algorithms of search engines. Your visibility or absence on the first page of Google search results can significantly affect your perceived credibility and authority in the real estate field, indicating a picture of prominence or obscurity.

The silent symphony of actions and inactions forms the backdrop against which your explicit digital engagements are set. It's the combination of the overt and the subtle that collectively composes the full digital score of a real estate leader's online presence.

KNOW: Assessing the Scope of Your e-Shadow

The first step in managing your digital footprint is simply to know and understand what's currently out there about you. This initial phase requires a comprehensive analysis of your digital presence and using search engines and social media platforms to obtain an unfiltered view of how you appear to the outside world.

Engage in a methodical search of your name, including the most common typos, and your titles, supplemented by your real estate niche, the name of your brokerage, or the specific real estate sectors you're connected with, spanning across all search engines (Google, Bing, Yahoo, etc.) to ensure thoroughness.

This step exposes the full scope of your online presence, revealing everything from professional milestones to personal moments that have found their way onto the digital stage.

To gain an unfiltered perspective of how the digital world perceives you, use incognito or private browsing modes, features available in most web browsers. This approach removes the personalization of search results, offering a clear, unbiased view of your digital footprint as it would be seen by someone encountering you for the first time online.

This step ensures you're not merely seeing a reflection shaped by your own online behavior but rather the raw results that are presented to the wider world.

Then proceed with an audit of your social media platforms. Begin with a critical assessment of your profile, profile pictures, and header images across platforms. These visual elements serve as the digital front of your persona; they often make the first impression online—before a word about you is read. Ensure these images are not only professionally appropriate but also convey a sense of your commitment to your real estate field, whether through imagery that resonates with your industry or a simple, dignified portrait that speaks of competence and trust.

Next, examine your handles and bio descriptions, as well as the content you've shared. This includes posts, articles, comments, and even likes. Each piece of content should align with your professional values, highlighting your knowledge, dedication to your work, and engagement with the broader real estate community. It's about more than just steering clear of potential pitfalls such as controversial statements or unprofessional behavior; it's about actively contributing to discussions and sharing insights that affirm your position as a thought leader and a reliable real estate professional.

Equally crucial is the scrutiny of your connections. Remember, the company you keep can impact perceptions of your professional judgment and affiliations. This is just as true online. Ensure your network includes only trusted friends and colleagues, industry leaders, and organizations that hold respect within your real estate niche. This not only bolsters your professional identity but also cultivates your feed with pertinent, current information, keeping you informed and actively engaged with the latest developments in your real estate field.

Continue with your virtual meetings setup. For real estate leaders today, these digital gatherings are not just a matter of convenience but also a critical component of business operations and team coordination.

As such, ensuring a professional appearance and environment during virtual meetings is just as crucial as in-person interactions. Consider the visual backdrop of your virtual meetings. A cluttered or distracting background can detract from the meeting's focus and diminish your perceived professionalism. Poor lighting can make it difficult for others to see you clearly, making communication less effective and potentially impacting the connection you're trying to establish. Audio quality is another critical aspect. Background noise can disrupt the flow of conversation and hinder clear communication. Use a high-quality microphone and consider wearing headphones to minimize external noise.

In the digital era, written communication forms the backbone of daily interactions. Beyond emails and text messages, real estate leaders engage in a myriad of digital correspondences, including project management tools, client portals, professional forums, and even comments on relevant online articles or blogs. Each platform and message carries the weight of your professional identity and requires careful consideration.

And always keep in mind that in the interconnected world of digital communication, the reach and permanence of your clicks and words extend far beyond the immediate recipient. Real estate leaders, entrusted with confidential information or representing their brands, must be especially vigilant. The potential for communications to travel unexpectedly is ever-present.

Emails can easily be forwarded, and a message crafted for a specific individual or group can quickly find its way into unintended inboxes. Social media posts, despite the illusion of control through privacy settings or the ability to delete them, carry the risk of being screenshotted and shared. Once something is shared publicly, or even with a restricted audience, there's no guarantee against the content being captured and redistributed by others. Even virtual meetings have the risk of being recorded without explicit consent. Third-party tools can capture audio and visual feeds, making any shared information, casual remarks, or discussions vulnerable to unauthorized distribution.

REPAIR: Correcting Your Cyber Image

This stage involves taking active steps to rectify or mitigate any negative aspects of your online presence—the "obvious problems." Whether it's unflattering comments, outdated images, misleading information, or more serious issues like unfounded allegations or the unauthorized release of information, taking decisive action is essential for maintaining your integrity.

When negative content is within your control, such as on your social media profiles, websites, or blogs, addressing these issues can be relatively straightforward. This could mean removing or editing the content in question or updating profile details to better reflect your current professional standing.

The challenge becomes greater when the adverse content resides on platforms or websites outside of your direct control. In these instances, the initial step is to contact the administrators or content creators, politely requesting the removal or correction of the content. Be clear about the content's negative impact on your professional identity.

If direct requests are unsuccessful, or if the content's removal is complex, it might be wise to engage reputation management professionals. These experts are skilled in strategies to de-emphasize negative content in search engine results, making it less visible or discoverable by those searching for you online.

During this phase, you should also confront the not-so-obvious problems. These are instances where the search results about you are not outright negative, but they don't adequately showcase your achievements or real estate expertise or the positive characteristics you wish to project. A search result that isn't damaging but also fails to showcase your qualifications or contributions to your real estate field can be equally limiting.

The strategy is twofold: enhancement and creation. Start by enhancing existing content. This may involve contacting administrators or content creators to suggest updates or additions that more accurately represent your professional achievements.

At the same time, focus on creating new content that truly reflects your professional identity. This can include publishing articles on reputable real estate industry blogs, participating in interviews or podcasts pertinent to your area of real estate expertise, or engaging in community initiatives that garner positive attention. Using social media platforms to share real estate insights, joining professional discussions, and highlighting your contributions can also greatly enrich the quality of your digital footprint.

Shaping the narrative around your digital presence is essential. Not only does it ensure your digital presence accurately reflects your real-world real estate skills and values, but also it establishes you as a thought leader in your real estate field. This proactive stance ensures that when clients, colleagues, or potential partners search for you online, they encounter a comprehensive and affirmative portrayal of your professional identity.

OWN: Claiming Your Virtual Real Estate

To address a potential problem, owning your name online is not just a matter of professional branding; it's a strategic necessity. A potential challenge arises when individuals share your name, a scenario not uncommon. From celebrities dominating search engine results to name twins with a more active online presence, these situations can dilute your digital identity, making it harder for clients or industry colleagues to find the real you.

To tackle this, it's crucial to establish a distinctive digital presence that clearly identifies you. This could involve using your middle name or initials in your professional profiles, incorporating professional titles or credentials, or choosing a unique version of your name that's linked to your area of real estate expertise.

These tweaks help ensure searches for your name lead to you, not someone else. Additionally, this acts as a safeguard against future issues.

The ever-changing nature of the internet means new figures can become prominent suddenly, potentially eclipsing your online presence.

For example, if a new celebrity with your name emerges, they could take over search results. Or worse, someone with a negative reputation could impact the perception of your shared name. Establishing a clear and unique online identity reduces these risks, keeping your professional achievements and reputation front and center.

This means going beyond merely setting up profiles on popular platforms such as LinkedIn or Instagram. It involves a comprehensive approach to claiming your name across all digital channels, ensuring you, and only you, control how your name is represented online.

The process begins with registering your name on as many social media platforms, professional directories, and relevant online forums as possible. Although it might seem daunting to maintain active profiles on each, the goal isn't necessarily to be active everywhere but to prevent others from assuming your identity or diluting your online presence. By owning your name on these platforms, you create a protective barrier around your digital identity, making it harder for others to impersonate you or misrepresent your professional brand.

Furthermore, secure your domain name (e.g., YourName.com). Even if a personal website is not in your immediate plans, having your domain is a crucial part of digital ownership. It blocks others from capitalizing on your name and sets the stage for a centralized space for your professional portfolio and contributions.

Also, delve into niche platforms and professional directories tailored to your industry. These channels enable you to claim your name in more specialized areas and improve your visibility amongst colleagues, acting as further validation of your professional identity and solidifying your standing within your professional community.

By taking these steps, you ensure that when you are searched for online, you present a consistent and controlled narrative, showcasing the breadth of your professional life, visible not only to clients or team members but also the wider industry network.

CONTROL: Commanding Your Digital Boundaries

Taking control of your digital presence extends beyond just owning your name across various platforms; it's also about meticulously managing the nuances of your online presence.

First, examine the privacy settings on all your social media profiles. Each platform offers a range of options that control who can see your posts, who can tag you, who can comment on or share your content, and even who can send you friend requests or follow you. It's essential to tailor these settings to suit your personal preferences and professional needs, ensuring your content is visible to the right audience while protecting your privacy.

Also consider the implications of your current connections because they can reflect on your professional persona. Be mindful of whom you accept or seek out because these connections can be viewed as an endorsement of your professional standards and network.

Moreover, be proactive in managing the content associated with your profile. Regularly review tags and mentions, removing or disassociating yourself from any content that doesn't align with your professional identity or privacy preferences. This might include untagging yourself from photos or asking colleagues to refrain from mentioning you in certain posts.

Additionally, think about the visibility of your likes, comments, and shares. These actions can be as telling as the content you post directly. They contribute to the overall narrative of your professional identity online, so it's wise to conduct these interactions with the same care and consideration you'd give to your own posts.

Finally, keep abreast of updates to privacy policies and settings on each platform. Social media sites frequently update their privacy features, and staying informed allows you to adjust your settings proactively, ensuring continuous control over your digital presence.

By taking these steps, you not only protect your professional reputation but also establish boundaries that respect your privacy and the privacy of those you interact with online. In an era where digital interactions can have real-world implications, such control is not just advisable—it's indispensable.

MONITOR: Persistent Surveillance of Your Online Self

The final step in managing your digital footprint is to vigilantly monitor your online presence. Regularly checking how you appear on the internet isn't an act of vanity; it's a critical component of professional reputation management. There's no harm and no shame in frequently searching for your name in search engines.

One effective strategy is to set up automated alerts. Most search engines offer this feature for free, sending you notifications whenever your name appears online. This proactive approach ensures you're always informed about your digital mentions, allowing you to address any new content quickly.

If you work in an real estate niche where client reviews and testimonials are common across search engines, social media platforms, general review sites, or industry-specific platforms, make sure to consistently review those too. Publicly expressing gratitude for positive feedback not only reinforces the favorable aspects of your services but also motivates others to share their experiences.

Addressing negative comments is equally critical. Prompt and constructive responses to less favorable reviews demonstrate your commitment to valuing client input and service improvement.

This approach is a chance to transform a challenging situation into a testament to your dedication to client satisfaction and service excellence.

In the fast-paced digital world, narratives can quickly spiral out of control if not addressed promptly. Being aware of what's being said about you online allows you to take timely action, whether it's correcting inaccuracies, responding to feedback, or updating your digital content to better reflect your professional identity.

And while it straddles a fine line in terms of privacy, keeping an eye on the digital activities of your team members can also be prudent.

Whether it's through email communication, virtual meetings, or interactions on various digital platforms, each digital touchpoint offers an opportunity for you to reinforce your professional identity. It's not enough to curate a strong social media presence or a professional website; every digital interaction must be approached with the same level of care and strategic thinking. This holistic approach to managing your digital professional identity not only safeguards your reputation but also amplifies the positive impact you can have within your real estate field.

Your look of leadership knows no bounds, it resonates through every pixel and screen and extends beyond the confines of your office walls, casting a digital silhouette as vast as your ambition.

Chapter 9
Leaders Lead by Example

By Changing Nothing,
Nothing Changes.

Chapter 9:
Leaders Lead by Example

Like a compass in the hands of a skilled navigator, a real estate leader's professional identity becomes the unwavering needle that points the way forward, steering their team through the challenges and uncertainties that lie ahead. A compass is a small but mighty tool, a symbol of direction, consistency, and reliability. It doesn't waver in the face of adversity, it doesn't bend to the whims of circumstance, and it doesn't falter in its purpose. It simply points north, providing a constant reference point for those who rely on it. In the same way, a real estate leader's professional identity serves as a steadfast beacon for their team, guiding them toward their goals with unwavering resolve. Your most paramount duty in your leadership role is to be that compass; but it's also to create more navigators who will be able to fulfill this role as well. It's about cultivating more real estate leaders—by demonstrating that exceptional leadership is less about dictating actions and more about setting a compelling example. By embodying the standards you wish to see, you become a real estate leader others are inspired to follow. This approach is what distinguishes a true leader from a mere manager. Whereas managers focus on ensuring tasks are completed and issuing directives, real estate leaders inspire action through their own choices. They don't just tell their team what to do; they show them how it's done. Your actions send a powerful message of "Do as I do," fostering an environment of mutual respect and emulation.

Great real estate leaders intuitively understand that leading by example is the most potent form of guidance that creates an unspoken standard: an organic dress code, a blueprint for behavior, a benchmark for communication, a template for digital engagement, and a standard for the living and nonliving elements that you surround yourself with in your environment that is far more influential than any written policy.

Your team members and colleagues are always observing, learning, and, in many cases, emulating your actions. Being a real estate leader means accepting you're always on stage, setting an example for every person you interact with. And although it might sound obvious, every moment of the day it's crucial, then, to ensure the example you're setting is a positive one. By practicing what you preach and paying attention to the minutiae of your professional identity, you not only enhance your leadership but also inspire your team to strive for the same excellence.

The flip side, being a poor role model, is the easiest way to undermine your own authority as a leader. Does that mean you have to follow all the rules (and burdens) your brokerage puts on you? Maybe. Does that mean you can't have your own style and can't stand out and show your personality? Absolutely not.

Influential real estate leaders are confident, and they trust themselves enough to live their own interpretation of a professional identity. They've put so much thought into it and created such a defined professional identity that their presence is instantly felt when they walk into the room. They're mindful of how others could perceive them and of how they want to be perceived by others. If part of this professional identity building requires leaders to wear denims, they wear denims. If wearing sneakers with their suit adds something unique to their defined professional identity, they wear sneakers. Influential real estate leaders exude confidence and trust in their ability to craft a distinct professional identity that resonates with who they are.

Courageous real estate leaders don't make excuses. They apologize when they've done something wrong. And usually people have the most respect for those who don't hesitate to say, "I'm sorry" or simply "I was wrong." But people have a hard time respecting those who look for excuses in advance. A real estate leader makes commitments, not excuses. If team members see commitment, courage, and taking responsibility for the actions and choices leaders have made, it feels safe and right to them to follow that person.

And the same is true for your team members. When it comes to their visual appearance, you too might be faced with a variety of excuses. Sometimes they claim it's too hot or too cold to dress appropriately, letting the climate dictate their professional standards. Financial concerns also play a role, with some feeling the pinch of investing in quality wardrobe items, or also grappling with guilt over spending. Time, that ever-elusive commodity, is another barrier, with the hustle of daily life supposedly leaving little room for meticulous planning. Amid these justifications, a deeper thread of resistance emerges. A claimed lack of style sense becomes a shield against change, and the actions of others—"They do it too"—serve as misguided validation. Geographic excuses, such as the claim "We're in the suburbs, not Manhattan," highlight a misunderstanding that professionalism has a zip code. Venturing into the digital world, some diminish the importance of a professional digital presence, dismissing it as "just the internet." This underestimation overlooks the profound impact of digital impressions in today's interconnected world.

These excuses, although varied, share a common theme: they believe that professionalism is confined to a specific weather forecast, price tag, or zip code.

As a real estate leader you might find yourself entangled in a web of excuses; and these justifications echo through the corridors, whispered by team members at all levels.

They observe their colleagues seeking loopholes in the standards that might justify their choices. In this landscape of justifications and rationalizations, your role as a leader becomes crucial. Successful leaders sidestep these excuses to send a clear message to their team members: professionalism is nonnegotiable, integral to the fabric of the brokerage, and essential for individual and collective success.

The Leader's Challenge: It's Not You, It's Someone Else

Sending a clear message to team members sometimes means having honest conversations with your team about sensitive topics that can range from inappropriate clothing to personal hygiene issues, from mismanagement of emotions to unfortunate social media posts, from neglecting workspaces to disrespecting clients. Although these discussions may feel uncomfortable, they're integral to maintaining the professional integrity your role demands. And it's not uncommon for leaders to feel apprehensive about raising such subjects. Do you? Maybe it's because of . . .

- Your commitment to fostering a positive team environment, knowing harmony is pivotal to brokerage success.
- An inclination to avoid causing emotional distress given your role, which may be centered on support.
- Concern over possible adverse reactions that could disrupt team cohesion.
- The need to exercise authority while maintaining a nonconfrontational stance to preserve team spirit.
- A tendency to avoid uncomfortable situations, particularly in a setting where team members work collaboratively.
- Finding the right words to express your concerns can be challenging.
- Thinking you are entering a personal space by addressing these issues.

However, remember that first and foremost, your goal is to support your team members' professional development, not to criticize them personally. Here's how you can approach these delicate conversations with confidence and clarity:

Begin by thoroughly preparing for the discussion. It's crucial to enter these conversations with a clear understanding of the issue at hand. Start by identifying the problem with precision. Reflect on the consequences this problem creates, not just for the individual involved but for the entire team, clients, and the brokerage as a whole. If it doesn't affect anyone, there's no need for a conversation.

Determine who is directly responsible for the issue. It's essential to pinpoint when the issue first arose and assess its frequency. Reflect on previous attempts to address the problem and their outcomes. This preparation helps you approach the conversation with a solid foundation, making it easier to discuss potential solutions effectively.

Finally, assess whether this is a conversation you should have independently or if it would benefit from the presence of another party, such as a human resources representative or a senior colleague. This decision should be based on the nature of the issue, its sensitivity, and the potential impact on the individual or team.

Get guidance before you approach. In any case, it's recommended you consult with human resources or a legal advisor if you have access to such a source, because some issues carry legal implications and require a delicate approach. Before diving into conversations about sensitive topics such as alcohol, drugs, religion, sex, violence, theft, fraud, harassment, or bullying, it's wise to consult with an expert. These experts can provide essential guidance on handling the situation correctly, inform you about any disciplinary actions that may be appropriate, and ensure you adhere to laws and policies.

Seeking such advice serves as a protective measure for both you and your brokerage. It helps prevent potential missteps that could lead to false accusations or lawsuits. Addressing such matters without proper preparation and understanding of the legal context could inadvertently cause significant harm.

Pick the best time and space. Selecting the appropriate setting for such a delicate conversation is critical, especially within the bustling environment of real estate offices or similar settings. These kinds of conversations should never occur in public spaces such as hallways, where there's a risk of being overheard or observed by others, compromising the privacy and dignity of the team member involved.

Instead, opt for a quiet, private space where confidentiality can be maintained—perhaps your office or a secluded meeting room. This environment ensures both you and the team member feel secure, don't get distracted, and are able to speak openly without fear of interruptions.

Additionally, choosing the right moment can significantly impact the receptiveness and outcome of the discussion. Avoid scheduling these talks during peak operational hours or just before or after stressful meetings, because stress levels and distractions can hinder the effectiveness of your message.

Instead, find a time when both you and the team member are least likely to be under immediate pressure, allowing for a more focused, calm, and constructive exchange. Also, you don't want to have to rush through this conversation because doing so could lead to misunderstandings or the feeling that the issue isn't really being taken seriously.

Bring yourself into the right mindset. Remember that these conversations are not personal attacks against your team member. Instead, they're meant to be constructive and help your team member, team, and brokerage improve.

Also, remember that neither of you is probably looking forward to this conversation. It's likely your team member is just as anxious as you are. So take a few minutes to clear your head and remind yourself of that objective.

Start the conversation off with positive reinforcement. This instantly reaffirms the value of your team member, especially if you share praise about measurable achievements. This could include citing specific instances in which their attention to detail improved transaction outcomes, their quick thinking averted a potential crisis, or their insights led to a significant increase in sales. Conversely, vague compliments like "You're doing great" or "We appreciate your hard work" lack the specificity needed to make the individual feel genuinely recognized. Such statements, although well-intentioned, fail to highlight the unique contributions of the team member and can, in the end, turn against you: "Well, you said I'm doing great. So what's the point?"

Focusing on concrete achievements sets a constructive tone, demonstrating you value their contributions in a specific area while allowing that there is room for improvement in another.

Use neutral and straightforward language. It's crucial to be clear and precise to ensure there's no room for misunderstanding. For instance, instead of saying, "Your outfits are inappropriate," you need to specify, "I've noticed that your wardrobe choices, particularly in terms of interaction with clients, may not align with our brokerage's expectations. This is especially true when you wear *xyz*." This approach makes your feedback not only more actionable but also less personal and focused on professional standards.

Aim for a delivery that is straightforward and unembellished, yet sensitive. Let the facts speak for themselves, and calmly present them without the distortion of emotional undercurrents. This ensures feedback is received as intended: as a means to maintain professional standards and uphold the brokerage's reputation, rather than as a personal critique.

Don't refer to others. When you need to address a concern with a team member, center the conversation on your own observations and experiences rather than on third-party comments or hearsays. It's crucial to base your conversation on incidents you've witnessed personally, not on anecdotes or grievances passed on by others. If the situation occurred in your absence, it's vital to have written, verifiable evidence to substantiate your points. This approach not only preserves the dignity of your team but also strengthens the trust between you and them.

Describe the consequences for them and your brokerage. Articulate the impact on their own reputation and the broader impact of their actions. For instance, explain how their choices not only hamper their own professional growth but also tarnish the collective reputation of the team, department, and brokerage. This perspective shift helps the team member understand the gravity of the situation beyond their individual sphere. For example, constant tardiness might not only affect their workload but also strain team dynamics and brokerage efficiency.

However, address these concerns without making it about your personal grievances (i.e., "I" statements). The focus should remain on the consequences of their actions on themselves and the brokerage, not on you as an individual leader. This ensures the feedback is purposeful and targeted toward fostering an environment in which their own well-being and the highest levels of brokerage excellence are maintained.

Be clear about how you would like them to change. Rather than dwell on the past, move on quickly to the future. But don't expect your team member to know exactly what you expect them to change. For instance, if a team member has been inconsistent in meeting client deadlines, don't just highlight past delays. Instead, clearly outline the steps for improvement, such as adhering to a time line for task completion, providing exact dates, and announcing regular progress updates.

Specify that these measures are nonnegotiable for maintaining the high standards of professionalism your team is committed to. Unless you're specific in your request, there will be confusion about what needs to be done (or not) moving forward.

Be careful when offering support. Although it's essential to be supportive, emphasize that the responsibility for improvement rests with the team member. You should be there to assist, but the obligation is on them. This stance prevents dependency and promotes accountability.

Be prepared for pushback. In fact, anticipate it—it's a natural response. However, it's crucial to maintain your composure and keep the dialogue centered on the matter at hand. Instead of allowing their response to sidetrack the conversation, seize it as a chance to emphasize your expectations and the importance of meeting them. Instead of leaping to defend your stance with rigidity, pause and truly hear what your team member articulates.

Misunderstandings, fear, or frustration often underpin their responses. This attentiveness not only demonstrates respect for their viewpoint but can also diffuse tensions, paving the way for a dialogue that's both more constructive and collaborative.

Although you can acknowledge their emotions as a way to navigate through their initial reactions, seize the moment to once again clarify the issue at hand, the solution you discussed, and the impact it otherwise has. By reiterating the conversation's objective—to foster their development and enhance overall outcomes—you underscore the collective aim of this exchange.

Remember, your conversation is not a personal critique from you, and similarly, their reaction is not a personal attack on you.

Summarize what was discussed and announce a follow-up. As you draw the conversation to a close, it's essential to encapsulate the key points discussed. This summarization isn't just about reiterating the issues at hand but also about confirming the mutual understanding and commitment to the agreed-upon actions.

It's a moment to ensure no detail is lost and both parties are aligned in their expectations and responsibilities.

Announcing a follow-up or a check-in at a specific date is the next critical step, one that underscores your dedication to the process, the individual's progress, and the overall success of your brokerage. However, this promise carries weight only if it's fulfilled. Failing to follow through not only diminishes the effectiveness of the initial conversation but also erodes your authority.

End the conversation on a neutral note. The way in which such a conversation concludes can significantly influence the subsequent actions and attitudes of your team member. It's essential to strike the right balance in the closing moments, ensuring the team member doesn't leave feeling overly discouraged or burdened by the discussion.

Conversely, ending on an excessively optimistic note might dilute the importance of the feedback you have given, a phenomenon I refer to as "sandwich" feedback: when the critical message is sandwiched between two positives, it potentially lessens its impact. Aim for a neutral closure, such as "Let's go back to work," which signals the discussion is complete and is just one of many interactions you have in your leadership role.

Document the exchange. This ensures there is a clear record, safeguarding both you and your brokerage against future misunderstandings or disputes regarding performance or conduct.

Start by documenting who was present during the meeting, capturing the full context of the discussion. It's vital to include the date, time, and location to anchor the conversation in a specific moment and place. This level of detail provides a foundation of transparency and accountability for all parties involved.

Next, meticulously record the substance of the meeting. What issues were discussed? This includes the initial observations that prompted the conversation, the feedback you provided, and the team member's response.

Crucially, detail the agreed-upon actions, including who is responsible for what and the time lines for these actions. This clarity prevents any ambiguity about expectations and responsibilities, ensuring everyone is aligned on the path forward.

Furthermore, outline the expected outcomes of these actions. What changes or improvements should result from this intervention? This sets a clear benchmark for assessing progress and effectiveness. Finally, specify the follow-up steps, including who will carry them out and when.

Documenting these aspects creates a comprehensive and indisputable record of the conversation. And this thoroughness underscores the gravity with which you, as a real estate leader, approach your role, demonstrating a commitment to fairness, transparency, and the growth of your team.

There may also be instances when you encounter a situation that falls outside your direct span of authority. Perhaps you're leading a real estate project with team members who don't directly report to you or you're in a matrix brokerage in which your influence is more lateral than vertical.

In this case, it's not recommended you have this kind of conversation. Instead, engage with the individual's direct leaders or with those who have the authority, sharing your observations and concerns—in the best case with documentation that underscores your concern.

To them, position your feedback not as criticism but as an opportunity for collective improvement, emphasizing the shared mission of providing exceptional real estate service. In these delicate scenarios, your role as a real estate leader is to facilitate positive change indirectly, using your influence to advocate for standards that align with the brokerage's values and objectives. It's a dance of diplomacy, requiring patience, empathy, and a strategic understanding of brokerage dynamics.

As you can see, leadership is a journey filled with challenges and responsibilities. It demands courage to engage in difficult conversations, wisdom to navigate the limitations of your authority, and the vision to see beyond immediate issues toward the greater goal of positive change.

In this journey, your professional identity is the compass that guides you and your team. It's the unwavering needle that points you north. When the terrain gets tough and the way forward seems uncertain, it's your professional identity that keeps you on course.

So, as you continue on your leadership journey, keep checking your compass. Make sure your professional identity is always pointing north. When you inevitably encounter obstacles and detours, use your compass to reorient yourself and your team. With your professional identity as your guide, you and your team can navigate even the most challenging of landscapes and emerge stronger and more successful than ever before.

Chapter 10
Moving Forward

If You Think You Can't,
Well Then You Can't.

Chapter 10: Moving Forward

In concluding our journey through leadership and the crafting of your professional identity, it's essential to recognize that enhancing your professional identity is not merely for personal gratification; it is a fundamental aspect of your professional development. This endeavor brings rewards that extend well beyond the surface. It influences trust within your real estate network, team cohesion, and opportunities for career progression. The critical question now shifts from whether you should refine your professional identity to the depth of your commitment to ongoing improvement and the pursuit of excellence. In the dynamic landscape of the real estate industry, where challenges and prospects exist side by side, the need to distinguish oneself for the right reasons is paramount. The capacity to set oneself apart through an outstanding professional identity is what differentiates the true real estate leaders. These leaders establish an identity that aligns with the values and goals of their brokerages, meets the expectations of their clients, supports the ambitions of their teams, and, of course, values themselves as the great real estate leaders they are.

This book has aimed to guide you through the nuanced dance of this professional identity, blending the science of first impressions with the art of a sustained imprint. From the subtle cues conveyed by your look to the profound influence of digital footprints. Many aspects of your identity have been dissected, offering you a blueprint for intentional self-presentation.

Now, about that potato chip on the cover. Did you notice?

At first glance, it may seem like a whimsical choice for a book dedicated to such a serious topic. Yet it serves as a powerful metaphor for the concept of identity—personal and professional alike.

Imagine, for a moment, we're embarking on a journey together through a bustling supermarket. As we navigate the aisles, our attention is drawn to the myriad of products vying for our attention.

The significance of packaging design becomes strikingly apparent—the strategic placement of brands, the few critical seconds that influence our decision to add an item to our shopping cart. It's in these moments that the familiarity of a trusted brand effortlessly convinces us to make a purchase, whereas the allure of a new product demands our notice through meticulously crafted packaging designed to leave a lasting first impression.

Consider, for a moment, the relationship between a product and its packaging. Although they are often perceived as separate entities, the most impactful packaging designs demonstrate that thoughtful packaging can not only complement but also enhance the product within. The packaging's shape, size, colors, and imagery are all chosen to sway your decision to buy or pass.

Now, let's pause in front of the snack aisle, and let's stare at the hundreds of potato chip packages in front of us. Chip packaging offers fascinating insights into successful branding. Did you ever realize every potato chip packaging has an image of a chip on the front? Did you notice how the most successful chip brands manage to communicate a clear promise: "What you see is what you get." The imagery shows perfectly shaped potato chips, which conveys the product's appeal more than any description could. It's straightforward, with no frills, showing the product in its most enticing form.

Yet there's a twist to this tale, as you know. The crumbled reality inside the bag doesn't match the perfection depicted on the outside. Despite not having a transparent section to preview the contents, we're drawn in by the promise of ideal, unbroken chips.

And not just once—again and again we continue to buy them, even if we're aware of the illusion.

The lesson here is profound: a compelling external presentation can lead people to embrace you, even if the internal reality doesn't quite match up (yet). Achieving the opposite effect is significantly more challenging.

For real estate leaders, the metaphor of potato chip packaging is a poignant one for the importance of a consistent professional identity. You must ensure your external presentation—your appearance, behavior, communication, digital presence, and work environment—reflects you in the best light.

Just as the chip bag's imagery promises a certain experience, real estate leaders must convey an identity that their teams and clients can instantly respect and trust. Although no real estate leader is without flaws—comparable to the mix of whole and broken chips within a bag—it's the strategic depiction of your competencies and commitment that should be emphasized. Over time, just as consumers come to accept the imperfect contents of a chip bag due to their trust in the brand, so too will others accept a leader's human flaws if they are convinced of the leader's dedication to their role and the success of the team.

Now let's take another look at the aisle of potato chips in front of us, and let's contemplate expectations. If I were to ask you to pick a spicy flavor of these chips, you'd likely subconsciously look out for a red bag. An organic variant? Green or brown.

Our brains are wired to associate specific colors and designs with certain product attributes. This principle of expectation extends beyond the supermarket aisle to the realm of leadership.

Just as we have predefined notions about product packaging, we also harbor expectations about a real estate leader's professional identity. Despite the diversity in leadership styles and personalities, certain universal expectations remain constant. Just as the bold red packaging of spicy chips stands out to a shopper looking for flavor, real estate leaders who align their presentation with professional norms are easily recognized and trusted.

There's certainly space for individuality and a break from convention, like a neon-pink chip bag among the typical reds and greens on a shelf. A real estate leader might also choose to deviate from traditional visual cues through distinctive clothing or an unconventional approach. This differentiation can attract attention, drawing those intrigued by novelty and signaling innovation. However, it may also miss the mark of subconscious expectations, posing a challenge to immediate recognition as a real estate leader in their professional field. Much like a shopper instinctively reaching for the familiar red bag, oblivious to a pink option, people often gravitate toward the comfort of what they know—traditional emblems of authority and expertise.

Finally, like well-established potato chip brands that are strategically positioned at eye level on shelves to be easily seen and chosen, influential real estate leaders naturally command a presence and often enjoy higher recognition, similar to products occupying premium shelf space. Conversely, less prominent brands—or real estate leaders—might need to exert more effort to be noticed.

In a competitive environment, being at eye level signifies remaining at the forefront of your managers' and all stakeholders' minds, always ready to be selected for your visible dedication to excellence, professionalism, and service. This prominence isn't merely physical; it extends to the entire professional identity you construct as a leader.

As this chapter closes, let the lasting lesson be the craft of your professional identity—the external manifestation of your inner capabilities. Let the professional identity you create stand as your unwavering representative, conveying expertise, fostering trust, and managing the intricacies of leadership with poise.

Your "packaging" is not merely an aesthetic choice; it's a strategic tool that, when aligned with your skills and vision, can weather the storms of challenge and change. Let it amplify your strengths, not overshadow them.

As you move forward, may your professional identity resonate with intention, your leadership echo with impact, and your presence be felt even in silence.

Stand out not just to be seen but to make a difference, to inspire trust, and to drive progress.

Here's to the real estate leader in you—packaged to perfection, poised for greatness, and perpetually ready to turn challenges into opportunities.

Go forth and lead, not just with authority but with the magnetism of a well-crafted identity, one that's as compelling and multifaceted as the real estate leader within you.

Acknowledgments

To you, the reader:

Thank you for choosing a path that extends far beyond transactions and deals. Every day, you navigate the complex landscape of real estate, driven not just by the pursuit of success but by the profound understanding that your work shapes lives and communities. As a real estate leader, you are the architect of dreams. You guide families through the emotional journey of finding a place to call home, a sanctuary where memories are made and futures are built. You are the catalyst for business growth and economic development. The properties you manage, the spaces you lease, and the investments you facilitate become the stages upon which entrepreneurial dreams are realized. You drive the backbone of our economy. The warehouses, factories, and distribution centers you develop and manage are essential for the supply chains that keep businesses running and communities thriving. And let's not forget the profound influence you have on the future of our cities and towns. Through your work in urban planning, land development, and community revitalization, you shape the very fabric of our society.

The decisions you make today will echo through generations, defining the spaces where people live, work, and thrive. Amidst the noise of disruption and innovation, you remain the human touch, the guiding hand that navigates the complexities of this industry. Your ability to adapt, to learn, and to grow ensures that the heart of real estate keeps beating, no matter how much the world around it changes.

To the real estate leaders who mentor and guide aspiring professionals, who share their wisdom and experience generously, thank you. Your investment in the next generation of real estate leaders is shaping the future of this noble profession.

And to the real estate leaders who balance the demands of their roles with their commitments to family and friends, I see you. Your ability to juggle multiple priorities and still bring your best self to your work is nothing short of admirable.

As you close this book, remember that your impact as a real estate leader extends far beyond the pages of a contract or the keys to a property. It's etched in the smiles of families as they step into their new homes, in the successful launches of new businesses, in the seamless operation of industrial supply chains, and in the thriving communities you help to build.

Never underestimate the power of what you do. You are the weavers of dreams, the catalysts of change, and the guardians of the spaces we call home.

With deepest respect and admiration,
Sylvie di Giusto

About the Author

International keynote speaker Sylvie di Giusto brings her expertise from a successful corporate career in Europe to every presentation. Formerly the head of a management academy and innovation hub, she developed innovative leadership programs for high-end education with unprecedented training methods. As the chief of staff for the chief human resources officer of Europe's largest tourism and retail group, Sylvie coordinated all group-wide human resources teams and activities. Prior to that, at a consultancy firm, she implemented online and in-person training and development initiatives for Fortune 100 companies. Now, respected organizations around the world—including American Express, American Airlines, Hilton, Nespresso, Microsoft, Prudential, and even the US Air Force—trust Sylvie to help them make the right decisions that grow their brands and bottom lines. Building on her five cornerstones of modern emotional intelligence—visual, behavioral, verbal, digital, and social—Sylvie gives her audiences the "Power of Choice," a conscious decision-making framework that allows us to understand our perceptions, choose our behaviors, and determine our best outcomes.

Sylvie is the author of *The Image of Leadership*, *Discover Your Fair Advantage*, and the upcoming *Make Me Feel Important*. Sylvie takes audiences on an entertaining, spectacular, and thought-provoking journey through the brain and mind and from the unconscious to the conscious—and ultimately to the heights of personal, professional, and organizational success.

For speaking engagements, contact Sylvie's wonderful team at: sylviebookings@cmispeakers.com, or call +1-403-398-8488.

Perception Audit

Take the free Perception Audit and unveil the image you project to the world in just 15 minutes. Receive a personalized report that illuminates how others perceive your professional identity, and learn to align your self-view with the impression you intend to make.

Are you ready to meet the YOU that everyone else sees?

Or visit sylviedigiusto.com/audit

After you've gained the clarity you need to polish your professional identity and project the very best version of yourself in the workplace and beyond, let's stay connected! Follow me on social media to join the conversation about *The Image of Leadership for Real Estate*.

- instagram.com/sylviedigiusto
- linkedin.com/in/sylviedigiusto
- facebook.com/sylviedigiusto
- youtube.com/c/sylviedigiusto
- tiktok.com/@sylviedigiusto

Your Voice and Our Collective Reach

Books—just like you—face perception challenges.

In a world where perception is reality, nowadays the value and impact of books are often judged by the quantity and quality of their Amazon reviews. So if this book has offered new perspectives or valuable insights, please consider sharing your experience online. Your review not only helps shape the book's impact but also guides others to find the same resource you did.

Your role in this narrative could just be the beginning.

For those who have found resonance within these pages and wish to spread the wisdom within their team or organization, I offer preferred customer pricing for bulk orders. Please reach out to my wonderful team at sylviebookings@cmispeakers.com, or call +1-403-398-8488. Let's empower more leaders together.

Made in the USA
Middletown, DE
30 October 2024